AF488268

12 Years in Labor

Give Birth to Your Purpose

CINDY CASIMIR

Copyright © 2023 Cindy Casimir

ISBN 9798218300852 (hardcover)

All rights reserved. No part of this book may be reproduced, stored, or transmitted by any means—whether auditory, graphic, mechanical, or electronic—without written permission of both publisher and author, except in the case of brief excerpts used in critical articles and reviews. Unauthorized reproduction of any part of this work is illegal and is punishable by law.

CONTENTS

ACKNOWLEDGEMENT

To my remarkable blended family,
My beautiful, imperfect, and wonderfully complex family.
Words prove insufficient to the profound bond that unites us.

In our shared existence, we've weathered storms of trauma, navigated the dysfunction, and shared tears as well as laughter, prayers, and countless meals. We are the mosaic pieces that together form the portrait of our family—a portrait enriched by the presence of everyone, by the shared experiences that have shaped us.

Our journey together has been marked by bends and little tears, yet these imperfections only serve to enhance the richness of our story. Without each unique member, our family puzzle would remain incomplete, lacking the colors and contours that give it life.

Furthermore,

To all those who stood by me when I couldn't stand myself, who showered me with genuine love and unwavering care, who recognized me even before I recognized myself, and offered wisdom and guidance when I was adrift—your impact has been immeasurable. You are cherished and hold a unique place in my journey of transformation.

And yes, even to those who sought to hinder my progress, attempting to shatter my spirit—your presence too played a role. In overcoming your challenges, I found a resilience that has propelled me to where I stand today.

In other words: "My haters were my motivators!"

"Through fractures, light finds its way,
In vulnerability, strength holds sway.
The scars we bear, the battles we've won,
In our brokenness, a new journey begun."

- Cindy Casimir

DEDICATION

This is a dedication to the wounded souls, the ones who walk the path less traveled, the hearts that ache in silence, and the spirits that have weathered life's storms. To those who have felt the weight of mistakes and regrets, who have been cast aside and deemed unworthy. This is for you, the ones who have been branded by society's judgments, yet possess a resilience and depth that few can fathom.

During your struggles and imperfections, do you realize the remarkable strength you hold? Your scars, your vulnerabilities, they are not symbols of weakness, but badges of honor. They are a testament to the battles you've faced, the mountains you've climbed, and the darkness you've conquered. It's through your fractures that your light shines brightest, illuminating a path for others to follow.

Embrace your authenticity, for it is a force that cannot be restrained. When you stand in your truth, you become a beacon of hope for those who tread in shadow. Your story, with all its twists and turns, has the power to mend the broken, to uplift the downtrodden, and to ignite a fire of transformation. You are not defined by your past; you are shaped by the courage it took to rise above it.

As you stand on the precipice of your own potential, know this: there is no chain that can bind you, no judgment that can define you, and no doubt that can deter you. You possess a strength that defies the odds, a resilience that defies expectations. The world may try to paint you with its limitations, but you are a canvas of endless possibilities.

This dedication is a reminder that you are not alone in your journey. You are part of a tapestry of souls who have faced the shadows and emerged with a radiance that cannot be dimmed. You are the embodiment of hope, a testament to the human spirit's ability to rise, to heal, and to shine.

So, let the world see you, unfiltered and unafraid. Embrace your story, your scars, your dreams. Your existence, with all its complexities, is a symphony of strength and vulnerability, a melody of triumph over adversity. May these words breathe life into your spirit, offering solace to the weary and kindling a flame of possibility in the hearts of the broken.

With unwavering belief,
Cindy Casimir

INTRODUCTION

When one contemplates labor, the natural association is often childbirth I, too, share this sentiment. Additionally, I envision a diligent individual toiling relentlessly, putting in hours of work for a meager fraction of their daily wage. My thoughts drift to Adam, banished from the Garden of Eden alongside Eve, and the solemn words spoken by God to him (Genesis 3:17 NIV; "Cursed is the ground because of you; through painful toil you will eat food from it all the days of your life."). However, upon delving deeper into the word's definition, several interpretations resonated with me profoundly:

- "Struggling to accomplish something despite earnest efforts."
- "Exerting one's physical or mental faculties with arduous and strenuous exertion."
- "Enduring adversity, distress, or burdens."
- "Striving diligently to effectuate or achieve a desired outcome."

These definitions compel me to acknowledge that life itself embodies labor—life is an arduous labor. Many individuals have encountered their distinct versions of labor: some have given birth, stepping into their purpose, and reaping the rewards of their toil, some may never discover their purpose at all. Then there's me—I remained oblivious to the labor I was undergoing. These are glimpses of the laborious moments that tested me physically, spiritually, and mentally. Be it monumental or minutes, these instances contributed to the sense of urgency in birthing my purpose, and the revelation of a greater calling bestowed upon my life, derived from the painful labor I endured.

There was a period in my existence when self-loathing consumed me, a profound shame for who I was. Consequently, I never truly unraveled my authentic self. I yearned to belong, to fit in somewhere—anywhere. In my pursuit of acceptance, I diminished my essence and tolerated a relentless succession of abuse, criticism, and judgment. In surrendering my innate power, bestowed upon each of us at birth, I lost my voice. I embraced countless fallacious narratives regarding my identity. I was a fractured, wounded child, striving to navigate my way, but without my voice, I failed to nurture the vulnerable child within me, allowing others to exploit her. While certain moments shall be illuminated in detail, while others are summarized to illuminate subsequent occurrences, and still others shall be reserved for a potential future tome.

Although I won't delve into the entirety of my life's narrative, sharing these experiences proved to be an immense challenge for me. Nevertheless, having granted myself forgiveness, I came to realize that part of reclaiming my voice is recounting the difficult tales—the ones that rendered me most fragile. Such tales are not exclusive to me; everyone harbors their own. While many choose to conceal them, there are those who unabashedly embrace them. The distinction lies in my newfound lack of shame and my resolute decision to invite you into this realm. It is my hope that, having perused these pages, you shall summon the courage to revisit the moments when you too neglected your inner self, and in doing so, rekindle the fire to speak once more, write once more, dream once more, hope once more, love once more, and simply live once more.

ONE

Sunny Miami, Florida, was our birthplace and hometown for my two sisters and me. My second eldest sister, Audrey, was born in Haiti and unfortunately never acquired US citizenship. My memories of her were limited to the times when our mother took us to visit her in Haiti. As I grew older, occasional phone calls were made, but back then, I could only speak what I call "broken Creole," and our conversations were brief. Our home resembled the house on the hill—it was the first house one would see upon entering the neighborhood, and our yard felt as vast as an acre when we raced through it. Melissa and I shared a room, while Esther, the oldest, shared one with our grandmother who moved in with us. I don't recall her arrival vividly; it's one of those memories akin to falling asleep on the couch and waking up the next morning in bed, with that lingering thought of "How did I end up here?" There are moments from my childhood that I often reminisce about, like climbing the mango tree and relishing the sweet and savory taste while perched on the back fence. My younger sister and I would make mud pies and even attempt to dip our cat into the kiddie pool (a mischievous act, I admit, but I desperately wanted her to swim). We would attend carnivals, walk to the corner store, you know, days when chips were only 25 cents per bag, and I'd splurge because I had a dollar in hand. However, when it came to my mother, I struggle to recall having a typical mother-daughter relationship—the kind where she would tuck you in at night, bake cookies together, play and read to you, or exchange those cherished words of "I love you." Of course, there were moments when we interacted; I remember one instance when she took me to work with her, and I sat there watching her type. But besides those fleeting instances, I felt as though I never truly got the chance to know her. I had so little to rely on, often feeling like a stranger observing from the sidelines. Before we moved to the house on the hill, we resided in what could be described as a duplex home. This memory also involves my mother vividly. On a chilly morning, she waited with me at the bus stop while I kept complaining about the cold. Our home was just down the street, so she hurriedly went to grab me an extra jacket. However, a few seconds after she left, the bus arrived. I let everyone go ahead of me, hoping to buy more time, but soon I found myself facing the bus driver. When I looked back, all I saw was fog. Finally finding my way to a window seat, I spotted her jogging back, her face filled with disappointment. Looking back now, I, too, felt the same disappointment. I should have waited for her. Sometimes that image resurfaces in my mind—the look on her face. Was that our "mother and daughter" moment, and did I miss it?

Then there was the instance when I didn't want to go to school. I can't fathom the reason behind my resistance; all I recall are fragmented memories, or perhaps just the fragments that left the deepest pain or anger. I found myself in the living room, and somehow, I must have provoked her because she forcefully pushed me out the door. As a skinny little girl, it felt as though she propelled me all the way to the bus stop, or in this case, our metallic porch door. The impact caused my lower lip to split, filling my mouth with a pool of blood. It was during this incident that my insecurity about my full lips began to take root, as I started to believe she had somehow made them appear larger. Despite the injury, she still insisted I attend school! Whenever asked about it, my go-to response was, "I fell off my bike," even though I didn't own one. I couldn't help but notice my mother's turbulent dating life. I struggle to recollect a time when it was just the two of us. She lacked a stable relationship with my father, as well as Melissa's father. Esther's father had passed away when she was young, and I, too, had an inconsistent relationship with my own father, who played no recurring role in my life. In retrospect, I believe my mother may have feared being alone. As I grew older, this observation influenced my own relationships with men. You see, as a child, what you witness often shapes your own behavior, since she didn't guide me on matters of womanhood. My observations became my teacher, but we'll delve into that later.

My mother had a penchant for capturing moments in our living room. She would dress up, meticulously do her makeup and hair. My favorite of her looks was a long, sleeveless black dress that shimmered as she walked. It exuded elegance, and her red lipstick added a touch of allure. In that very living room, I would immerse myself in the music playing on the stereo, acting out the lyrics. It wasn't mere dancing; I would embody the songs, truly feeling them, much like a soundtrack playing in the backdrop of films. A few details from my school days still stand out in my memory: the black and yellow uniforms, my favorite class being Haitian Creole, and my lack of close friends due to my extreme timidity. I also endured taunts for not yet growing into my full lips. However, I managed to become a safety guard, proudly wearing a yellow badge. I cherished that badge, particularly because a fellow guard and I were selected to appear on the morning news, educating others about the importance of carrying the badge. I was undeniably nervous, knowing the entire school would see me. Thankfully, the librarian provided us with the script, and I remember gazing at the immense camera, feeling a sense of awe as I had never seen anything like it before. Once the filming began, my fears dispersed. Lastly, the cafeteria doors presented as a challenge for a fourth grader like me. As I mentioned earlier, I was a lanky and slender child. Frustrated with my constant struggle to open those doors, I started doing push-ups the night before, determined to triumph and enter the cafeteria without a sense of defeat.

My mother had an on-and-off boyfriend named Al. There was a strained relationship between Esther and Al. I vividly recall one night when I feared Esther might stab him. In the hallway, my mom and Al were engaged in a heated argument with Esther holding a knife. Instead of harming anyone, she plunged the knife into the wall, tears streaming down her face, smudging her eyeliner into dark streaks. Sometimes, I wish I had paused to embrace her. I knew so little about her, yet somehow, I understood why she couldn't always be there for us. Considering Esther's absence from home, I can recall one night when I woke up, intending to check on her. However, as I pulled back the covers, all I found was a heap of clothes in her place instead. It was perplexing how often they clashed, even though Al consistently tried to protect me. I have one memory that remains fragmented—a day when things spiraled out of control, and my mother chased me with a knife. Al stepped in, attempting to shield me from her. Another incident occurred when I brought a not so fridge worthy report card home. She had the belt ready to discipline me, but once again, I clung to the back of Al's shirt as he managed to deter her. I don't recall many interactions with Al, apart from him often claiming to be my father. I never corrected him because, at least in his eyes, someone desired that title.

Al always wanted us to go out together as a "family," and we would take the bus to an amusement park called Bayside. He had children of his own, Dede and Ricky. Some days, they would stay with us, sharing a room. Due to my fear of the dark, I would sleep with Dede, unknowingly opening the door to an even greater darkness.

TWO

One morning, Dede forcefully placed her hands in my pants, guiding me to put my mouth on her breasts. I felt uncomfortable, but my mouth and body froze. Every single time, I couldn't muster the strength to move or find the words to speak. I simply went along with it. In hindsight, I wish I had been a stronger-willed child who could have said "NO!" It began as a morning routine but quickly escalated to nightly encounters. Dede was around sixteen years old, and her brother, who may have been as young as fifteen, eventually decided to join in. Underneath the covers, Dede would instruct him, using only his fingers. If it wasn't my turn, he would focus on "pleasuring" Dede. They made it seem natural, as if they had done it before. There were times when I pretended to be asleep, yet I would still be awakened.

Esther used to tell me that our mother worshipped the devil, which was not considered unusual in Haitian culture. We didn't attend church, but I found myself drawn to reading the Bible and watching Sunday sermons. Looking back, I recall that my mother had a separate room within the den. The room would contain untouched food, adorned with pictures on the walls and candles. This explained the chills I felt whenever I entered that room. Esther would inform me that my mother hosted dinner parties for these demons. I have faint memories of dressing up for these occasions but now with the understanding of the true backstory.

I briefly met my father for the first time and stayed with him, only to discover that his house was just a few buses away. I had several siblings from my father's side. In that area, there wasn't much to do, so some of my siblings and I resorted to engaging in a playful activity of tossing rocks at each other. Taking positions at our respective bases, we would dodge the incoming projectiles. It was an enjoyable game until I witnessed a swiftly hurled rock heading straight toward me, moving too fast to avoid. The impact knocked me off my feet, and I felt blood trickling down my neck. I realized that the rock had caused a gash on my chin that I still feel today. To alleviate the swelling, my brother placed a quarter on the wound. However, our father eventually noticed, and they faced the consequence of his belt.

One of my brothers always treated me to ice cream whenever we heard the familiar sound of the truck outside. He kept an empty jar hidden behind the couch, filled with the money he had saved. He was my favorite sibling, until one evening when he took me to a secluded area in the living room and began kissing me in places, I didn't think boys were supposed to see. He insisted it was my turn and proceeded to remove his pants, pressuring me to perform an inappropriate act. Just as I felt trapped, my sister walked in, and I hastily fled the room. Next day after school, when the bus stopped at my mother's house, I found myself rising from my seat. Melissa was playing outside and welcomed me with a warm hug, making me realize how much I missed home. I no longer saw my father, and Al, or his children when I returned. I didn't inquire about what had happened, I was simply relieved.

Unfortunately, upon my return, my mother's health started deteriorating. It began with her spending her days confined to bed, never leaving her room. Esther dropped out of school to start working. With my grandmother being elderly and unable to provide much supervision, we found ourselves with limited guidance. Melissa and I would play outside until the sun went down, and it was during one of those evenings that we noticed a new family moving in across from us. Soon after, Katie's mother came over to introduce herself and her daughter. From that day on, the three of us became inseparable. We spent most of our time at Katie's house, where she had the latest toys, and her mother would always prepare dinner for us. Katie's father we didn't see often, but when we did, he was kind during our interactions.

When Katie visited our house, we would take advantage of our spacious backyard, running laps and playing tag. In Miami, there was a free bus that we could take to go places, and we loved taking it to visit Esther at her workplace or, my personal favorite, the supermarket Publix. Armed with our backpacks, I would play the role of the mastermind, instructing Melissa and Katie to discreetly select whatever treats they desired, and we would then make a thrilling getaway, returning home with bags full of sweets.

One night, the two of us decided to play "house." Without realizing the implications, I unintentionally replicated the abusive behaviors I had experienced, passing them on to Katie. I would assume the role of the father, and Katie would portray the mother. We reenacted the hurtful actions carried out by Dede, Ricky, and my brother, as it felt like that's what a "family" was supposed to do. Unbeknownst to me at the time, this was one of my greatest regrets, perpetuating the trauma I had endured.

The final year we spent in Miami coincided with the last time we saw Katie. Melissa and I were drawn to the window by the flashing blue and red lights. Opening the door, we found the police outside their house. We rushed over to see Katie and her mother in tears, with her father in the back seat of a car. Katie's mother had bruises on her face. Shortly after that incident, I recall her mother packing their belongings and loading them into the car. We didn't reach them in time, as Katie was already seated in the back when her mother drove away. Standing on the sidewalk, we could only gaze at each other in disbelief, knowing that we would never see each other again. It was just Melissa and me once more. Occasionally, we would still go to Katie's house, sitting on her porch, reminiscing about our shared memories.

During my mother's illness there were moments when I thought she was getting better. I remember coming home one day to find two dresses hanging above my bed. Excitedly, my mother entered our room and asked if I had seen them. I stood up and ran my fingers through the soft, silky fabric. The dresses were sleeveless and fell to my knees. I nodded. In retrospect, I wish I had said more to her. However, as I grew older, I accepted the reality of our strained relationship, and I no longer yearned for that bond. I assumed she would always be there. That belief was shattered when the ambulance arrived at our house once again, rushing her to the hospital. Soon, my mother began staying at the hospital more than at home. I don't recall many family members or even Al visiting during that time. It was just us, navigating through this challenging period on our own.

While she was away, I didn't attend school as frequently. So, when my mother returned, I turned to Melissa and whispered, "I wished she had stayed at the hospital." Little did I know those would be the last words I uttered.

It was January, Friday the 13th. I was in class when my teacher distributed journals for us to write in. She mentioned that her mother was also sick, which led me to pen the words, "I wish my mother and her mother felt better." Strangely, writing that down gave me a sense of hope, relieving some of the guilt I felt for my previous wish. On my way home from school that day, I eagerly anticipated reaching my house, even though a slight uneasiness lingered in the air. As I finally arrived, I found Esther and my grandma standing in the living room. Before I could even close the door completely, Esther burst into tears, and deep down, I already knew what my heart refused to accept. She was gone. I walked over, and we held each other, overcome with grief. From that moment on, everything became a hazy blur.

Melissa's dad started to visit more frequently, and Esther took charge of arranging the funeral. It was during this time that I was introduced to my uncle and his family, I remember my uncle's two daughters, Gaina and Abby. Abby was just a baby at the time, while Gaina was closer to Esther's age. Gaina's beauty is something that stood out to me. I recall sitting next to her in the limousine on the way to the funeral service. Her brown, doe-like eyes were captivating. I remember her holding a white flip phone, which briefly distracted me during the journey to the service. We traveled in a limousine to the funeral, and during the ride, I absentmindedly played with my white ruffled socks, running my fingers through them. Thoughts about those dresses crossed my mind, wishing I had spent more time with my mother, engaged in deeper conversations, and discovered more about her. My thoughts led me to another memory when she wouldn't let me leave the table until I finished all of my Mayi Moulen (Haitian cornmeal). Luckily, my princess PJs had pockets, so

I stuffed the cornmeal into them. After being dismissed, I hurried to the bathroom and flushed it down the toilet. She might have noticed the weight difference in my pockets, or maybe she did and let me off the hook because of my creativity. My thoughts were interrupted as the limousine came to a halt. It was time to confront the painful truth. The funeral was attended by unfamiliar faces, and time seemed to slip away rapidly until the final moments arrived for us to bid her a final farewell. Standing beside her casket, adorned in a blue suit and her signature red lipstick, she appeared peaceful. At least her suffering had come to an end. Afterward, Melissa's dad brought us food, but my appetite had vanished. All I wanted was to wake up from this never-ending nightmare. Unfortunately, the next morning it was confirmed that there was no escape. I recall entering her room one last time, gazing at her empty bed, reminiscing about the moments when I would lie there and watch TV. On her wall, there was a newspaper cutout of the singer late Aaliyah. My mind drifted back to the time when Melissa and I discovered our Christmas presents on the top shelves of the closet.

As time passed, Esther continued to care for us. Soon, the devastating Hurricane Katrina struck, and suddenly Esther asked for our opinions on moving to Pennsylvania to live with our uncle. Curiously, I kept asking if they had stairs, although I couldn't quite grasp why it had become a priority on my wish list. Before we knew it, Melissa's dad took us shopping for suitcases, and we found ourselves preparing to be dropped off at the airport. Since Melissa's father had not been a consistent figure in her life, there were no tears shed from her side.

THREE

I was 12 years old when my mother passed away. I didn't fully comprehend what was happening, and I didn't know how to process it. It felt like my world had suddenly changed, and everything happened so rapidly that I couldn't determine if it was for better or worse. My emotions were in a state of confusion and pain, which eventually led to anger directed towards myself and my mother. I never had the opportunity to express or truly absorb the weight of my experiences because I brushed them off and the swift transition didn't provide much time for reflection. Being a shy person and considering that open expression of emotions wasn't common in our household, I struggled to understand the multitude of feelings that were swirling inside me.

I must emphasize that my uncle not only took a risk but also made a tremendous sacrifice by welcoming three additional girls into his home, despite already having children of his own. Of course, as a young child, I didn't fully grasp the significance of his actions. As I grew older, Esther shared with me my uncle's backstory. She told me about how he immigrated to America from Haiti, built a new life, and endured his own childhood traumas. He faced a difficult relationship with his family, including our mother, as they too participated in mistreating and rejecting him. Learning about this shed light on why my mother never mentioned him and the challenges they faced in their relationship. Perhaps it was hard for him to accept me, seeing a reflection of my mother in me. Especially since there was animosity between us, I felt overwhelmed with guilt, fearing that I was no different from my mother due to the way I treated him. It took time for me to realize that both of us were operating from a place of trauma during that period in our lives.

Our uncle picked us up from the airport, and during the ride, I relished the opportunity to admire the new surroundings. It was a mix of awe and attachment to what we had left behind. While part of me felt like I was leaving my mother, I found solace in being with my sisters. As we finally arrived at our destination, the neighborhood revealed its beauty, and everything felt refreshingly different. The house exuded warmth and a sense of welcome as we stepped inside, filling my heart with excitement, especially at the prospect of exploring the renowned stairs. However, my excitement was continued by the sound of footsteps racing down the stairs. It was Gayu, radiating pure joy and love, but she spoke so rapidly that I couldn't comprehend her words. I was particularly happy for Esther. It meant she could experience a more "normal" teenage life, free from the burden of mothering her younger siblings.

As the commotion continued downstairs, I slipped away, with Meme quietly following me up the stairs. I found amusement in the sound of each step creaking beneath my feet as I ascended. However, my exploration came to a halt when I found Meme already in tears. Being the youngest, I had never considered how challenging the transition must have been for her. Feeling helpless, all I could do was hold her tightly and assure her that at least we were together. Eventually, I guided her to the bathroom to rinse her face, leaning against the doorway as we heard the echoing announcement, "Mom's home!" from the bottom of the stairs to the bathroom. I exchanged a glance with Meme and gently took her hand as we prepared to greet our aunt.

Our aunt was a gentle soul, with kindness emanating from her every word and gesture. She moved through life with grace, and Meme instantly grew attached to her. It wasn't long before we began attending school. I found myself repeating the 5th grade, while Meme and I went to the same school, conveniently located within a short walking distance. School had never been something I looked forward to. In Miami, I had grown to dislike it, and I wasn't sure if I would have a similar experience at this new school. Over time, rebellion and resentment started to take hold of me. I still clung to the idea that we might return home at any moment. In Miami, I had never been intentionally disobedient to my mother or shown her disrespect, even in an unhealthy environment. However, at such a young age, it was difficult to fully comprehend the reasons behind my emotions. Losing my mother became the tipping point, causing all the pent-up frustrations to overflow. In a way, I wished people understood the underlying pain, but it often came across as a deliberate choice to be difficult or ungrateful. This sense of being misunderstood only grew stronger.

The first act of defiance occurred when I disobeyed my aunt, and Gayu promptly made me walk up and down the stairs 100 times along with writing "I'm sorry" in French. In an instant, my fascination with stairs vanished, replaced by a bitter taste of consequences. In the mornings, Esther and Gai would already be off to school, leaving me with the opportunity to sneak into Gaina's closet. I couldn't resist admiring her collection of clothes and choosing a shirt or a pair of shoes for myself, without her permission, of course. Most of the time, I'm unsure if she noticed my little secret or perhaps, she did notice but chose not to mention it. Perhaps that's what led her to surprise me with my first Hollister shirt for Christmas, a brand that might have been overrated but was trendy for someone my age, and I wore it every chance I got.

My curiosity often led me to explore her belongings - flipping through photo albums, tinkering with her piano - her life fascinated me because it appeared so wonderfully "normal" in my eyes, she swiftly became a role model, standing tall right alongside Esther.

Melissa and I would walk together, enjoying our time together until we reached her classroom. However, one morning, my daydreaming in class was abruptly interrupted by the sound of my name being called over the loudspeaker, instructing me to report to the front office. All eyes turned towards me, their gazes making me feel as if I had committed a crime. With my heart pounding louder than my footsteps, I made my way to the office, where my aunt was waiting for me. Her expression spoke volumes before she even uttered a word. She informed me that I would be leaving early. My immediate concern was for Meme, and I anxiously asked, "Where is Meme?" Silence filled the room, and I repeated my question, hoping for a different response. In a calm and whispered tone, my aunt replied, "Her dad took her back to Miami." Tears welled up in my eyes and streamed down my face. How could he take her? He had never been present in our lives while we were in Miami, and now he had taken away my best friend, my partner in crime. It was another unexpected blow that left me devastated. I couldn't help but think about that morning when I had walked her to class, realizing that we had never exchanged the words "I love you." When I returned home, everyone was already waiting for me. In an inexplicable impulse, I picked up the phone and dialed her father's number, a number I didn't even realize I knew until that moment. After several attempts, I finally dialed the correct number, and a voice with a deep accent answered. "Who is this?" the voice asked. I hesitated for a moment before responding, "It's Cindy! Can I speak to Melissa?" There was a brief silence on the other end, followed by a trembling and soft voice. "It's Cindy, Meme!" her voice breaking as much as mine. Despite my desire to ask her countless questions about where she was and what was happening, the tears prevented me from forming the words.

I withdrew into myself, seeking solace in solitude as I grappled with the whirlwind of emotions swirling inside me. The months passed by, and summer arrived, bringing with it an unfamiliar sense of loneliness. I had never been alone before because I always had Meme by my side. Though I did spend more time with Abby, I found myself nurturing a bond with her. It's a peculiar twist of fate, considering that I had lost one sister while gaining another. Occasionally, my aunt would drop me off at Barnes and Noble, where I would immerse myself in the world of books. Apart from that, the memories of that summer are hazy, as if they vanished in an instant, and before I knew it, 6th grade was upon me, unleashing a wave of rebellion

I found a friend in Nikki, a girl who lived in the same neighborhood, not too far from home. We would walk after school together, much like Meme and I used to do. During our walks, we often encountered a boy named Brad, who lived a few houses down. He would strike up conversations with me, despite being in a higher grade. One day, I didn't want to go home yet, so I sought refuge at Nikki's house. Her mother greeted us warmly, and as I entered Nikki's room, I was captivated by its resemblance to a miniature mall, reminiscent of Katie's room. I sat on her bed while she changed out of her school clothes, and that's when my gaze fell upon her struggle. Her hoodie had become entangled with the necklace she was wearing. Moved by an impulse, I stood up to help her, but my attention was abruptly drawn to her arms. They bore multiple cuts, and I couldn't tear my eyes away from them. Caught in the act of staring, I felt a mix of curiosity, concern, and fear. Sensing my unease, Nikki reassured me, "It's okay, just don't tell anyone." Just then, her mother called us, informing us that dinner would be ready soon. As she closed the door behind her, Nikki rolled her eyes and whispered, "I hate her." My heart shattered into pieces as she began to explain that when she feels stressed or upset, she resorts to self-harm as a coping mechanism. The idea of inflicting pain upon myself sounded unbearable, yet she reached under her bed and retrieved a pencil box. As she opened the lid, I discovered it contained an assortment of razor blades and band-aids. With great care, she selected a blade from her collection to demonstrate her chosen method of release.

She gave me instructions on how to handle the razor and prepare my arm. With swift motion, she made a clean swipe across her inner arm, her demeanor unfazed, as if it were a routine. Blood began to trickle down slowly, but she didn't rush to clean it. She stared at it for a moment, captivated by its presence. It intrigued me, but I couldn't fathom myself doing the same. Realizing the lateness of the hour, I abruptly understood that I had to make my way home. As I reached my driveway, a sense of dread enveloped me. Without a moment to gather my thoughts, I entered the house, and there was my uncle sitting in the living room. Keeping my head down, I tried to pass him and head for the stairs. However, he halted me, inquiring about my whereabouts. My mind raced, struggling to concoct a plausible lie. Finally, I mustered, "Stayed after school." Uncertain whether he bought my explanation, I hurriedly ascended the stairs, relieved to evade further interrogation. Thus, it became my daily routine—spending time with Nikki, growing closer to her, and returning home to face the same questions.

Once, I arrived home a bit later than usual, and as expected, the interrogations commenced. This time, however, it escalated into an argument. Instead of retreating to my room, I made the impulsive decision to leave. I wandered aimlessly for what felt like an eternity, and upon my return, I was met with a startling sight—the police waiting for me. My uncle opened the door, aware that I had only worsened the situation. After their departure, I made my way to the kitchen, only to be met with rage from him. I couldn't contain my anger and shouted back; he grabbed me and forced me to sit atop the deep freezer and struck my thigh with such force that I had to bite my lip to suppress the tears. "I'm going to F you up, isn't that how you talk now-a-days?" Filled with confusion and rage I pushed past him and raced upstairs. Consumed by anger and frustration, I sought solace in tears, my pillowcase soaking them up as I struggled to regain control of my breathing. Determined to calm myself, I splashed cold water on my face in the bathroom. My eyes locked onto my reflection, and to avoid prolonged self-reflection, I opened the mirror, revealing the contents of the medicine cabinet. Among them, a razor sat on the middle shelf, tempting me. Every voice inside me urged me to take it, and without further hesitation, I did. I rinsed it off, breaking the plastic barrier that shielded the blade. Hesitant but resolute, I swiftly executed my decision. Surprisingly, the pain was not as intense as I had anticipated. In fact, it served as a distraction from the overwhelming emotional pain I was experiencing. With each subsequent swipe, I became increasingly numb to the sensation. To conceal my actions, I resorted to wearing long-sleeved clothing, playing the part of someone untouched by the darkness within. Now, I understood why Nikki engaged in such self-destructive behavior.

Curiously, I never confided in Esther, who seemed focused on her studies, and making friends at school. I didn't want to burden her with my troubles. However, it wasn't long before cutting myself became a regular occurrence. One day at school, during a routine physical examination, the nurse requested that I raise my hoodie higher. I immediately refused. When I returned home later that day, my uncle, Gayu, and Esther were waiting for me, their concerned faces etched with worry. They ushered me to the rocking chair, creating an atmosphere of solemnity. Finally, I mustered the courage to reveal my secret. I confessed that self-harm had become an outlet for me, a way to temporarily escape the turmoil within. Despite their good intentions, the intervention they staged did not yield the desired outcome. Looking back, I am uncertain of what could have truly helped me during that dark period. They probed, asking why I resorted to such drastic measures, reminding me that they didn't engage in such destructive behavior. But my response, uttered through tears, remains vivid in my memory: "I am not Esther or Gayu."

FOUR

Okay, let's take a moment to process everything that has unfolded so far. It's crucial to understand that I don't intend to portray anyone as a villain in this narrative nor myself as a victim. During that period, I was grappling with deep-seated trauma that my family was unaware of. I carried emotional baggage, and in a traditional Haitian household, concepts like self-harm were unfamiliar and challenging for them to comprehend. Unfortunately, the weight of everything I had experienced from the ages of 8 or 9 until I was 12 started to consume me. Despite my genuine desire to be a carefree child again I resulted to acting out or being disobedient, it seemed no one truly understood this longing, and it was easier for them to label me as a girl with an attitude problem. This misjudgment became ingrained in people's perception of me, exacerbating my sense of isolation and fueling my anger towards everyone.

However, a turning point emerged when my guidance counselor, Ms. Hall, took an interest in me. It was the first time I opened to someone about the real reasons behind my relocation to Pennsylvania. I confided in her about my self-harm and the incident involving my uncle. I expressed my profound longing to be with my mother back in Florida. Finally, it felt liberating to share the thoughts that had been swirling inside my head. Our counseling sessions became a regular occurrence, providing a safe space for me to delve deeper into my emotions.

Soon, rumors spread throughout the sixth-grade body, and I became a target for bullying. I endured hurtful names like "psycho" and "emo girl." Some individuals even doubted the authenticity of my cuts, labeling me as the "marker girl." When I confronted Nikki, seeking support, she dismissed me and distanced herself. So, I found solace in skipping classes with my guidance counselor. She would personally collect my assignments from my remaining classes, allowing me to spend most days in her office.

February 28th.

Instead of being in class, I found myself having lunch with Ms. Hall. Birthdays never held much excitement for me, so spending it outside of class to enjoy pizza wasn't all that bad. I had planned to return to class afterward, but Ms. Hall had a different idea. She mentioned that she wanted me to meet someone. Just then, he walked in—a middle-aged man wearing round glasses, dressed in a suit, with a dainty briefcase in one hand. He extended his hand to shake mine. "This is Neil. He's from Children and Youth," it took me a moment to grasp the situation. "He's going to be your caseworker," she continued, explaining that he would be responsible for finding me a new home.

Tears streamed down my face as the realization of leaving Esther hit me like a wave. She assured me that Neil would accompany me home so I could gather a few belongings. Conflicting emotions surged within me—I felt betrayed and overwhelmed with guilt. This wasn't the outcome I wanted. If only I had known, I would have never spoken up in the first place.

Easton.

Neil drove me home, assuring me everything would be okay. When we arrived, only my aunt's mother was at home. As I walked through the door, I could see the tears in her eyes. She kept repeating in Creole, "What did you do? What did you do?" I couldn't find the words to respond; tears just continued to roll down my cheeks. I didn't even have a chance to say goodbye to everyone. I entered Neil's SUV with my belongings stuffed in a trash bag, and I kept my gaze fixed on the house until it disappeared.

Neil attempted to engage in conversation, but I was too distraught. Overwhelmed by emotions, I eventually fell asleep during the long ride. When we arrived at our destination, Neil explained that this place was just temporary until he could find me a permanent home. It was a cluster of buildings interconnected, resembling a campus. As I stepped inside, I was greeted by a cacophony of voices—children talking, laughing, and crying. Some were older, while others were younger. Neil escorted me to the office where a woman with a stack of paperwork and a barrage of questions awaited. He handed me his card and told me to reach out if I had any problems.

Amidst the glass-paneled walls of the office, devoid of any other people, the woman completed my intake process. She asked about my birthday, and I replied, "Today." She mustered a cheerful, "Oh, happy birthday!"—the only birthday wish I received that day. She then guided me to my room before closing the door curiously, I asked her where I was, "The Children's home of Easton," she replied with a smile.

Inside the room, there were three other girls who remained silent. I took it upon myself to explore the surroundings. Just around the corner, I discovered more rooms. Mine was tucked away in the corner, near the end of the hallway. Peering inside, I found a dull, blue-painted room with a solitary bed. The windows were fitted with sturdy bars, making it impossible for me to open them even if I tried.

That night, lying in bed and staring at the ceiling, tears streaming down my cheeks, I uttered my first prayer. Filled with fear, I asked God to protect me. As soon as the words left my lips, I felt as though He was in the room with me, and I drifted off to sleep, finding solace in that presence.

I didn't officially attend school there. They would only open the door to bring us food and some worksheets, but they were never checked. I remained in Easton for a few months or so.

Valley Youth House.

Neil informed me he had found another place for me to stay. Despite our limited conversations, he always showed kindness and made sure I was okay. He mentioned that he would provide me with a clothing voucher once I settled into my new home. This news excited me, as I hadn't been able to bring much with me from home.

Neil explained that he was still working on finding the "perfect" permanent home for me. In the meantime, he took me to a shelter called Valley Youth House. It was smaller than Easton but didn't feel as confined. Unlike Easton, there were planned activities and outings during the weekends, offering some variety to our daily routines. Although I still wasn't attending school, they had teaching sessions in the basement, designed like a classroom, where I could continue my education. I stayed at Valley Youth House for a longer duration compared to my time at Easton.

Being There.

After spending several months at the shelter, Neil informed me that he had found a home for me in the Poconos called Being There. It was quite a distance away, but as we entered the neighborhood, I was amazed by the size of the houses. The scenery around us helped me remember my surroundings, as most kids do. Surrounded by mountains, the area was peaceful and quiet as we drove through each street. Finally, we arrived at the last house, perched on a hill.

A tall, slim, older woman was waiting for us with the warmest smile as we pulled into the driveway. Neil told me to go inside while he grabbed my bag. The pathway to her door felt never-ending. As she opened her arms for a hug, I didn't hug her back, but she was still more excited than I was. "I'm Nina!" she exclaimed. Finally letting go, she eagerly showed me around the home.

The entrance greeted us with a beautiful glass chandelier, and there was a grand wraparound staircase to the side. The living room was breathtaking, and the kitchen was the largest kitchen I had ever seen. There were five bedrooms in total, including Nina's, and it was the first time I saw a Jacuzzi in a bathroom. I was in such a daze that I didn't even hear Neil say goodbye. Nina took me out to eat that night and told me to order whatever I wanted, and that's exactly what I did.

During our conversation, Nina opened to me about her passion for starting a group home after years of waiting. She had always had a soft spot for helping young girls. It was too late for me to enroll in school at the time. However, she assured me that after summer was over, I would be attending Stroudsburg Middle School. One of my favorite activities was walking around the neighborhood, admiring the beautiful homes. Soon, another girl named Tiff arrived at the home. Nina took both of us on outings and made sure we stayed productive. I would often take Tiff with me on my walks, showing her my favorite houses.

One night, Tiff confided in me that she was planning to run away and asked me to keep it a secret. As she packed her things and silently left, I peacefully laid in bed as she snuck out the window. Eventually, summer came to an end, and school started. It was uncomfortable being the only black girl in my classes, and I struggled to make friends. The school was enormous, and after having lunch, I would retreat to the library to feel less awkward sitting alone. Afterwards, Nina would always wait for me at the bus stop, which, in an odd way, reminded me of my moments with my mother.

FIVE

Valley Youth House (Again)

After some time at Being There, I attended my first court date, where I would see my uncle to have his parental rights discussed. It was during this time that I was introduced to my child advocate. The courthouse was filled with a variety of people—mothers crying, men in handcuffs, security guards, officers, and guard dogs. It was a chaotic environment. Sitting on the top floor, looking out the window, I spotted my uncle, and it felt like ages.

Before entering the courtroom, my advocate asked me if I liked where I was living and if I wanted to go back. In that moment, I froze. It was my chance to go back with my uncle, to see Esther again. But no answer came out of my mouth. When my uncle was posed with the same question by the judge this time, a part of me secretly hoped that he would stand up for me, that he would fight and voice his thoughts. However, reality didn't align with that wish. He relinquished his parental rights without much of a struggle or second thought. At that moment I was okay with staying with Nina. My advocate spoke on my behalf, considering I was a minor. When it was all over, I felt a sense of rejection and abandonment by him. I got over it, because I saw Nina as a mother figure, I had become attached to her. It was just her and me, and maybe I was trying to recreate a relationship I had never experienced.

But none of that mattered when, after just a couple of months, Neil picked me up early from school. It felt like I was reliving the pain of losing Melissa all over again. All I remember him saying was, "You won't be going back to Being There." My heart broke, and the only thing I could ask was, "Why?!" It was probably the first time I raised my voice towards him. He paused and explained, "I did my best to keep you there, but Nina didn't have the proper paperwork she needed." He continued, "You'll be going back to Valley Youth House until I find you a new home."

I was filled with anger. I didn't want to go back to Valley Youth House; I wanted to return to Nina's home. But it didn't matter. Neil took me straight to VYH, and my frustration grew. I couldn't shake the feeling of wanting to go back to the warmth I had found at Nina's. Nevertheless, I had to accept my current situation and hope that Neil would find me a similar home.

Later that week, Neil did come, but we weren't going back to Being There. He had found a home for me in Mt. Erie. Honestly, my time there was short, and I can't remember the woman's name. She was an older woman and once again, I was the only girl in the house. On my first day, I tried to give it a chance. She had me attend weekly group sessions where we were expected to participate and share our trauma. However, I didn't want to do that. I found myself surrounded by other kids in the system, and I would mostly listen to their stories. When it was my turn to share, I remained silent.

I had to attend these group sessions twice a week, and as she was getting ready to take me, I refused to go. She insisted that it was mandatory and helpful, but I wasn't interested in hearing that. I locked myself in the bathroom and wouldn't come out. I was desperate, looking for a razor to harm myself. Frantically searching through her medicine cabinet, I was lucky enough to find one. But before I could proceed, she forcefully opened the door with her body, snatched the razor out of my hand, and prevented me from causing any harm. I ran upstairs and locked myself in her room, sitting on her bed, feeling overwhelmed and distressed.

Suddenly, everything escalated. Four policemen arrived and started breaking down the door. They restrained me, and it was my first time experiencing a 302, (a.k.a involuntary psychiatric commitment.) Two of the officers pinned me down and placed me in handcuffs. Weighing only about 90 pounds, I was picked up by the arm and put into the back seat of the police car. I was terrified, believing that I was being taken to jail.

Horsham Clinic.

Instead of arriving at a prison, we pulled up to a mental hospital, and Neil was already waiting for me. I could sense the disappointment on his face as he sat with me during the intake process. Guilt washed over me because I knew he didn't want to be there so late at night. As always, before leaving, he handed me his card and urged me to reach out if I needed anything. I asked him how long I would have to stay there, and he responded, "That's up to you." His words echoed in my mind as I entered the facility.

Horsham Clinic resembled Easton in some ways, with a mix of boys and girls. The hallways were straight, lined with multiple rooms on each side. Inside each room, there were three beds and a shared bathroom. My roommates were Brandy and Jackie. They gave their reasons for being there. Brandy shared that she had been in foster care for various reasons and had ended up in Horsham after attempting suicide. Jackie, on the other hand, disclosed the sexual abuse she had endured from her father and her own struggles with self-harm. Hearing their stories was heart-wrenching, but it also made me feel less alone in the emotions I was experiencing.

Being at Horsham was a turning point in my treatment journey. It was there that I was prescribed antidepressants and sleeping pills, even though I initially doubted their necessity. The sleeping medication left me feeling drained most of the time. There was no way to avoid taking the medications as they closely monitored our intake. Nearly everyone in the facility was on some form of medication, and staff members always made sure we swallowed them. We were under constant observation, with staff supervising us even when we were given something as simple as pencils. Every request had to be made, whether it was for necessities like tampons.

The atmosphere at Horsham was a mixture of strict monitoring and an underlying sense of camaraderie among the patients. We were all facing our own battles, and despite the challenging circumstances, there was a glimmer of comfort in knowing that others understood the pain and struggles we were going through. Yet, alarming on how many young boys and girls conducted self-harming attempts.

Recently, I came across an investigation regarding the use of psychotropic drugs for foster children. Some alarming statistics caught my attention. Children in the foster care system were administered powerful mind-altering medications thirteen times more often than children who were not in care. It's crucial to consider that many of these children have already experienced trauma, neglect, or abuse. By resorting to medication as a first-line approach, we are essentially conveying the message that the present version of these children is too difficult or troubled for us to handle. We are numbing their valid emotions and bypassing their needs, without fully considering the potential long-term side effects.

Before resorting to prescriptions, it is essential to acknowledge the real underlying problems. These children need a loving home, a listening ear, understanding, a sense of worthiness, and acceptance. We must recognize that the root of their struggles lies in their environment and experiences. It is far more crucial to address those issues than to rely solely on medication. The studies mentioned in the investigation even pointed out that some of the medication combinations prescribed to these children were considered too risky for adults. ADULTS! Maybe you should reread that part again.

It is distressing how easy it is to label these kids with conditions such as depression, ADHD, or bipolar disorder without taking the time to truly understand their circumstances. Just imagine if every time you, your spouse, boss, co-worker, or best friend had a bad day or went through a difficult time like grieving the loss of a loved one or experiencing a breakup, they were immediately labeled as depressed or bipolar. Can you picture a daily delivery of antidepressants and other medications showing up at their door? Moreover, government officials enforcing the medication regimen, convinced that it is the *only* best solution for them to function better?

Personally, I never believed that I was depressed or bipolar. I was defiant and misbehaved due to past traumas. At that moment, what I needed was not medication; I needed my mother or a nurturing figure whom I could trust. It is crucial for us to question the immediate reliance on medications and consider alternative approaches that prioritize the emotional well-being and healing of these children.

Reading these findings has opened my eyes to the complexity and potential harm that can arise from an overly medicated approach. It reinforces the importance of seeking comprehensive solutions that address the root causes of the children's struggles, rather than simply treating the symptoms. By providing them with the support, love, and understanding they deserve, we can truly make a positive impact on their lives. Okay now back to regular programming.

We had our usual med calls at the nurse station, and in a classic moment of comedic timing, I found myself triggered and attempted to pull off a daring escape from the clutches of medication. Looking back, it could have been an early stage of self-sabotage or perhaps the meds were playing tricks on my mind. Who knows?

As it was my turn to approach the glass window, I seized the opportunity for distraction. I waited for the nurse to put my meds into the cup before swiftly throwing her off balance with an unexpected request for a tampon. Caught off guard, she turned around, and with my twiggy arms, I skillfully slid through the opening, snatched the medication bottle, and swiftly crammed as many pills as I could into my mouth.

Well, let's just say chaos erupted faster than a squirrel running off with a stolen acorn. The nurse slammed the alarm, and before I knew it, staff members were converging on me from every angle, tackling me to the floor like I was auditioning for an avant-garde interpretive dance routine. I was promptly whisked away to the isolation room, where I found myself strapped down and placed on a 72-hour suicide watch.

Being left alone with my thoughts aside from my personal entourage of staff members following me everywhere I went, whether it was to the bathroom or for a shower. It felt like I had my own reality show, they were the camera crew, and I was the unwilling star.

But amidst the craziness, there was Mr. Dan, the wise and supportive voice amid my madness. He always told me that I was destined for greater things than "this place." As we sat together during lunch, he would embark on his motivational speeches. "You don't need to be here," he'd say. "You've been through a lot, but that's not a reason to end your life. You're going to grow into a talented woman who will inspire others. You can't do that here."

Now, I must admit, I didn't take his words seriously at the time. But looking back, I knew he was right about one thing—I didn't belong there. Despite the setback caused by my escape attempt, I had to keep moving forward. And so, after a few more eventful months, on my best behavior, I finally received the news I had been eagerly waiting for—I was being discharged.

And so, with a mix of relief, trepidation, and an oddly fond memory of my acrobatic pill-swallowing escapade, I bid farewell to the Horsham Clinic. The next chapter of my life was waiting, and it was time to embrace it with open arms, and hopefully fewer medications.

SIX

VYH (Third Time's the Charm)

According to Neil, I was about to become the first girl residing in the all-boys group home across from the shelter. Fortunately, this time I wouldn't be sent far away. The home was a two-story building with a basement serving as the laundry and pantry area. Upstairs, an open-concept layout encompassed the living room, kitchen, and dining table, creating a seamless space. A hallway led to the rooms, with the staff office and therapist situated in the middle, along with the director. During my intake, I received information about the staff I would soon meet, and they informed me that after summer, I would enroll in Log College Middle School for 8th grade. As part of our routine, we had a chore board and received an allowance every Friday upon completion. This became the longest period I had spent in a single home. The main reason for this was Ms. Jolie, who exuded a nurturing spirit that naturally drew me towards her. Despite initially feeling intimidated, the boys in the group home were generally welcoming and didn't bother me much. Steve, always eager to share his latest comic book read, and Zac, who was quiet yet prone to occasional bursts of temper. Lastly, Chris, the most talkative and open of them all, became someone I frequently conversed with. Gradually, I settled in quite well. The staff members were hospitable, and the atmosphere of the group home didn't feel overly institutionalized. We were still afforded certain freedoms, especially during the evenings when only one overnight staff member was present. This staff member allowed us to watch TV past our bedtime, and I occasionally stayed up late, joined by Zac. Things started off fine, and Zac continued to engage in conversations with me.

However, after being at the group home for slightly over a month, once again sexual assault found me. Overwhelmed by fear, it took me several weeks to confide in the staff member with whom I felt the closest connection. Sadly, after summoning the strength to share my experience, I don't recall any subsequent actions being taken, nor do I remember hearing anything further regarding the incident. After a few months, another girl named Angie arrived, becoming my roommate. Angie was kind-hearted, and we often stayed up late discussing our experiences with the boys. It marked a significant transition into the "teenage" stage, as we both attended the same school, with our sole shared class being an emotional support session. Thankfully, despite the challenges, I managed to make a friend and complete the school year without significant disruptions.

Shortly after, another girl named Lira arrived, and let me tell you, she was a rebel with a piercing obsession. It seemed like she wanted to pierce anything and everything she could get her hands on, including my tongue. Well, I guess the way my life has been all I was missing was a rebellious accessory.

Despite Lira's piercing adventures, I decided to make the most of my stay at the group home and aimed for the highest level of achievement. I was determined to do what was necessary to reach that status. But hey, what's life without a little self-sabotage, right? It wouldn't be me if I didn't indulge in some questionable decision-making at this age.

So, one night, the girls managed to talk me into going on a daring adventure to celebrate my upcoming birthday. We hatched a cunning plan to sneak out during the night shift of the staff. With precision and finesse, I kicked out the netted screen covering the window and embraced our taste of freedom.

Picture this: running through the fields, the wind caressing our faces, and the sound of our laughter echoing through the campus. It felt like we were starring in a thrilling movie, the mischievous heroes escaping from a group home to experience the wild side. It was like those crazy Miami nights spent running through my backyard with Melissa and Katie.

But as luck would have it, our moment of normalcy didn't last long. Just when we thought we were invincible, staff members appeared down the aisles of the store we had impulsively stumbled upon—none other than K-mart, the epitome of spontaneous adventures. It was like they had sixth sense for detecting escaped teenagers.

So, there we were, caught red-handed during our bold escapade. As we sheepishly climbed back into the van, the silence was almost deafening. But you know what? I couldn't help but crack a smile. Sure, it meant I would be demoted back down to level zero and forfeit the chance to enjoy my birthday to the fullest. Yet, it felt like a night out without a horde of watchful adults and the entire household while others stared at us like we were a variety box of trouble. It was a much-needed break from my norm.

Of course, as we returned to the group home, Kristen, one of the staff members who had accompanied us, didn't quite share our sense of adventure. Before we stepped foot back into the house, she took a moment to express her disappointment. She lectured me about almost being the highest-level resident and yet allowing others to talk me into regressing back to square one. Kristen insisted I should be more discerning about who I considered my friends and thoroughly think through the consequences of my decisions.

And so, amidst the chaos, I couldn't help but find humor in the situation. Who would have thought that a birthday celebration would turn into a daring caper at K-mart? It's funny how even unintentional patterns like never celebrating my birthday seemed to become a part of my unconscious routine.

Each self-sabotage I engaged in seemed to lead me up another treacherous stairway of life. Maybe it's just my past roots playing tricks on me, or the meds at this point, trying to keep me on unstable ground and constantly resetting my progress.

But hey, amidst all the chaos, I decided to join the cheerleading team. It was a step towards stability, a commitment that kept me focused and productive. As part of my newfound routine, I decided to meet with the therapist at the group home. She had this uncanny ability to dig deep and wanted to know everything about me on a personal level. Now, if you know anything about my history with confiding in adults, you'd understand why I approached this with caution. But you know what? Despite my reservations, I gradually opened to her. After all, those pesky thoughts of self-harm would occasionally creep into my mind, and it felt good to release that burden. Little did I know that within just one hour of pouring out my thoughts, I would find myself magically transported to a place called Foundations. I mean, talk about efficient transportation services!

And there you have it—a new chapter in my journey, all thanks to a seemingly innocent therapy session.

Foundations, Therapy Tales, and the Art of Speeding Up.

Foundations, another clinic like Horsham, was the place I never wanted to be. Despite my reluctance, I couldn't deny that it was at least cleaner and nicer than the previous one. They even had bigger rooms, stretching from the cafeteria to the TV area. As usual, we had group sessions where I preferred to stay silent, until the group leader handed me a journal. She instructed me to pour everything out onto its pages, from my thoughts to any random musings, and if I felt ready, I could share them with her. Little did I know that this was the moment my passion for writing was born. I fell head over heels in love with the written word and discovered my own talent. I started writing everything down, and soon enough, I found myself diving into the realm of poetry on a regular basis. Although I never shared any of it with the group leader, writing became my solace, helping me cope during my time there.

During one of my visits, Neil showed up. During that visit, he introduced me to my new worker, Megan, whose pixie-cut blonde hair immediately caught my attention. As she spoke about her plans for me, she also touched upon the possibility of adoption. Brimming with hope and determination, she seemed committed to finding me my 'forever family." Hearing those words filled me with excitement because, truth be told, I was exhausted from the instability. I continued to write during the remainder of my time at the clinic, always armed with a brand-new journal. Whenever I had sessions with my therapist, I couldn't help but put on my "everything's fine" act just to wrap things up quickly. But deep down, I couldn't shake the thought of how everything had come full circle. If I hadn't ended up at Foundations, would my hidden gift for writing have remained undiscovered? Or would I have stumbled upon it later down the road, like finding that elusive sock that always goes missing in the dryer? I mean, let's face it, Foundations wasn't exactly my dream vacation spot, but hey, sometimes life takes us on detours we never expected.

After spending time at Foundations, I was released for good behavior. Maybe all I needed was some time away. I returned to VYH, and Megan continued her frequent visits. We went out together, enjoying ice cream and sharing moments. Her genuine care and curiosity about me were evident, and she even gave me the affectionate nickname 'My Cindy girl.' Every time she saw me, she would use it, reminding me of my family's nickname for me "Cin Cin." Perhaps all I needed was a female worker like her. Megan took pictures of me for adoption websites, and together we awaited eagerly to see what the future held.

So, as I reflect on my journey, perhaps it was all part of a grand cosmic plan, carefully choreographed to ensure that I discovered my passion for writing at just the right moment. Who knows? Maybe one day, I'll write a bestseller about the misadventures of my therapy sessions, titled "Therapy Tales."

Gloria.

I spent a little over a year at VYH before Megan informed me that she had found a permanent home for me. It was a mix of emotions for me—part of me felt sad about leaving, but there was also a sense of relief. I was the last of the original group to leave, so on my last day, the staff organized a party for me. They created a poster filled with heartfelt messages from everyone. It was a touching gesture, and it made me realize that, for the first time, I had completed a full grade without any mid-year disruptions. As summer arrived, I prepared to leave VYH and start a new chapter.

Enter Ms. Gloria, the woman who became my new caregiver. She was nice, although she had a more traditional approach to things. I discovered that I was the first girl to live in her home. Ms. Gloria had specific rules about watching TV, so I found other ways to occupy my time—writing and going for walks. It took a while for me to determine how I truly felt about living there.

One day, Ms. Gloria asked me to clean the house. I wasn't in the mood for it, and we ended up having an argument. Eventually, my frustration reached its peak, and I couldn't resist the temptation of a classic act of self-sabotage. So, I walked out the door without knowing where I was headed. I entered a store and asked a customer if I could use their phone. I called Megan and expressed my desire to leave Ms. Gloria's home. Megan instructed me to ask the stranger where I was, and she came to pick me up. I made it clear that I didn't want to return, despite having been there for less than a month. She wasn't happy with me, as a result, Megan dropped me off back at the VYH shelter, which surprised everyone, including the staff from the group home. I stayed at the shelter for a few weeks until Megan found a temporary home for me to stay in during the summer with a woman named Ms. Ebony. She also mentioned the chance of a family in New Mexico or somewhere like that wanting to adopt me, and I was totally open to it since I was ready for a fresh start. On the day of my departure, Ms. Ebony came to pick me up from the shelter.

SEVEN

As we drew closer, I recognized the familiar sights of Levittown. Oh, the flood of emotions and memories that hit me all at once! As we passed Clara Barton, I caught a glimpse of the back of my uncle's house, and disbelief washed over me. It seemed like destiny had led me right back to where it all began.

Upon entering the home, I realized it was in the same neighborhood as my uncle's house. In fact, I was just down the street. Ebony showed me the room I would be sharing with Grace, another girl who was also there. She introduced me to her oldest son and his wife, who happened to be staying there at the time. Across from them, Wayne, Ebony's youngest son.

In my eagerness to understand the situation, I confronted Megan about not informing me that I would be in the same area as my uncle. But she explained that it was meant to be temporary, and she didn't want me to get too comfortable. I wasn't even allowed to visit my uncle's house unless my sister came to see me at Ebony's place. The plan was always to move on from there.

As the summer days passed by, Grace and I grew closer. It was just the two of us, navigating this new chapter together. Ebony took us on outings with her family, and Grace and I would stroll around the neighborhood. It felt surreal to be right back where it all started. Sometimes, I would walk past my uncle's house, wondering how he was doing and reflecting on the journey I had taken.

On some nights, when Ebony spent the night at her fiancé's house in Bensalem, it would be just Grace and me. Ebony provided me with a cellphone so I could check in. Slowly, our relationship transformed into a mother-daughter dynamic, and she asked me how I would feel if she adopted me. My heart leaped with joy at the thought. Just like that the plan was set in motion, even discussing it with Megan. Everything seemed to be falling into place as summer neared its end.

Looking back now, I can't help but wonder how my life would have unfolded if I hadn't chosen to stay somewhere familiar and kept searching for something else. I had been so hard on myself for leaving in the first place, thinking it was a second chance. But I was mistaken. I should have stuck to the original plan.

The honeymoon phase continued as Jason and his wife moved into their own home, and I eagerly settled into their former room downstairs. It was a moment of excitement to have a space of my own. Soon, another girl named Hannah joined our household. She was reserved and didn't speak much. Hannah and Ron, Ebony's brother, seemed to develop a close bond, which I brought to Ebony's attention. This resulted in Ron angrily confronting me later that night, hurling insults and demanding that I mind my own business. Ebony advised me to ignore him, so I retreated to my room. Things took a darker turn when Hannah threatened to harm me if I fell asleep. After some time, Hannah ran away, and it was through a Facebook post that we discovered she was with Ron.

Shortly after, another girl named Steph joined our group. I recognized her from school, it seemed like I had finally found a place where I didn't feel the urge to escape. Ninth grade flew by, and as summer approached, Steph and I were chosen to attend a leadership retreat for a week. However, my excitement was short-lived when Steph was caught smoking weed during the retreat. Ebony called us in for a meeting, asking if she should kick Steph out. In my frustration about the disrupted retreat, I reluctantly said "yes." Little did I know that answer would open the door to even more drama, orchestrated by Ebony to sow manipulation among us.

Grace's departure hit hard. She was adopted by another family, and it was clear that she didn't want to leave. Ms. Ebony had expressed her desire to adopt Grace, but perhaps things didn't progress quickly enough, and she slipped away. That was the red flag I failed to notice.

Now it was just Steph and me. We managed to get along for the most part, navigating the ups and downs of our shared journey. During this time, I landed my first job at Sesame Place, which required me to take the bus. One evening, after a late shift, I found myself in need of a ride home. I reached out to Ebony, but she was in Bensalem and wasn't inclined to come and get me. So, I decided to undertake the hour-long journey on foot.

It was during this walk that I realized I needed some guidance. I stopped by a bar to ask for directions, and to my surprise, a kind man offered to give me a ride home. I can't explain why I got into the car with a stranger, but in that moment, his kindness reassured me. However, he also took the opportunity to advise me against repeating such a risky decision. Looking back, I can't help but acknowledge the dangers I may have unwittingly exposed myself to when I shouldn't.

Wayne, started bringing his friends around, and among them was Brad, the same Brad I used to come across during my morning school walks with Nikki. It was nice to have familiar faces around. Including reconnecting with Gayu and Esther, seeing them filled me with a sense of joy and nostalgia.

One night, when the house was empty, Brad's visit took an unexpected turn. I didn't pay much attention at first, but he entered my room, and before I knew it, things escalated, and I found myself losing my virginity. It was a quick and unplanned encounter, and I didn't want to get into trouble, so I chose to keep it a secret, not sharing this experience with anyone.

As time went by, Ebony thought it would be wise for Steph and me to start using birth control. We went to Planned Parenthood and as part of the routine, they conducted a pregnancy test before proceeding. The nurse seemed to take longer than usual to return to the room, and when she finally did, she handed me a pink slip. Reading the words "5 weeks pregnant" on that slip sent my heart into a freefall. I was speechless, and the weight of the news pressed heavily upon me. Gripping the slip in my pocket, I settled into the backseat as Ebony drove us home, its presence feeling like it was drilling a hole into my leg.

Upon reaching home, I sought solace in my room, hoping that sleep would offer respite from the overwhelming reality I now faced. The following day, after school, I mustered the courage to approach Ebony for guidance and closure. To my surprise, her reaction was not what I had anticipated. "You can't live with me if you're pregnant," she declared, and my heart sank. The place I had come to consider my sanctuary suddenly felt like a dream. Instead of understanding, her response was laced with anger, leaving me shattered and uncertain about what lay ahead.

News of my pregnancy quickly spread, reaching Brad, unsure of how to proceed, I turned to my sister and aunt, seeking their counsel and support. It was during this time that Ebony revealed that Brad's father had offered financial assistance for an abortion. Although part of me knew it wasn't the path I truly desired, confusion clouded my judgment.

Despite the advice from my aunt and sister to keep the baby, I still felt trapped by the fear of leaving. Even though both Brad and Ebony were against me having the baby, my heart was resolute. I was determined to go through with it. Megan presented a plan for me to enter a "Mommy and me" program, essentially a group home for teenage mothers. However, she made it clear that it would be located far from Levittown. This sparked a new wave of thoughts and doubts. Did I really want to bring a child into the system? Was it fair to subject my child to the challenges I was still grappling with? Ebony constantly reminded me that she wouldn't adopt me if I had the baby, further complicating my decision-making process. Feeling confused and conflicted, I ultimately chose to have an abortion.

The building where the procedure took place had an unsettling appearance, and the presence of protesters outside only added to my unease. Brad accompanied me through the process, and I filled out countless forms on a clipboard, answering endless questions. But as I sat in the room surrounded by other girls, something within me shifted. Sitting beside Brad, I mustered the courage to express my hesitation. I walked out of the room and found solace on the curb outside, with Brad following closely behind. He uttered words that ignited a surge of anger within me, saying, "If you keep this baby, I want a DNA test." I fought back the overwhelming urge to unleash my hands on him, despite never disclosing to him that it was my first time. We called Ms. Ebony, and her furious reaction made it seem as though she believed my body belonged to her. She repeated that if I kept the baby, I couldn't stay with her, and she wouldn't adopt me. Also informing me I would have to leave immediately.

Emotionally drained and constantly hungry, I started to grow distant from Ms. Ebony, feeling the warmth in our relationship fade. In my moments of uncertainty, I found solace in the company of Jackie, a friend of Ms. Ebony's. Jackie would share with me the things Ms. Ebony said behind my back. She revealed that Ebony had initially considered adopting me but changed her mind upon learning about my pregnancy. This revelation became the tipping point for me. I yearned for Ebony to adopt me, to finally be part of something stable.

I turned to Jackie for support and guidance, and she suggested revisiting the abortion clinic. In a state of emotional turmoil, I acquiesced, hoping it would be the best decision for me. On the day of the appointment, Jackie picked me up in her truck, and we made a stop at her house where Brad was present. I barely uttered a word, consumed by my thoughts and inner turmoil. Jackie handed me a bottle of water to soothe my upset stomach, but moments later, I vomited it all out. Throughout the car ride, anxiety gripped me tightly. I knew deep down that this wasn't what I truly wanted, but it seemed like the only viable option for my adoption. We arrived at the clinic, greeted by the familiar faces of protesters urging me to reconsider. Gathering my resolve, I forced myself out of the car and entered the building, where another stack of paperwork awaited me.

Once the paperwork was completed, I was led to a secluded area in the back. The hallway was painted in a shade of green, with a few girls dressed in hospital gowns sitting silently on benches. A nurse approached me for another consultation, explaining the procedure and its implications. Overwhelmed by a mix of emotions, I remained silent, unable to make eye contact. Eventually, she handed me a gown and guided me to a room where I could change. I caught a glimpse of myself in the mirror and felt a profound sense of shame. In that moment, I slammed the toilet seat down and took a seat, clutching the gown tightly in my hand. Tears streamed down my face as I whispered, "I'm sorry," directing my words to the tiny life within me. Placing my hand on my stomach, I mustered the courage to stand up and remove my clothes. Wiping away my tears, I stepped out into the hallway and found solace on a bench, keeping my distance from the other girls. Nurses would periodically appear and guide the girls to their respective rooms, and they would vanish for hours, leaving behind an unsettling void.

My heart continued to race, pounding so forcefully that it felt like it might burst out of my chest. In that moment, I almost wished for that physical release. Suddenly, a gentle hand rested on my shoulder, startling me from my thoughts. "Cindy?" The nurse's voice reached my ears, accompanied by a soothing smile. Shaking my head slightly, I realized it was time. Nervously, I followed her into the room. Inside, a male doctor and two other nurses awaited me. The room had an eerie resemblance to those seen in scary movies. It was spacious, yet my attention was fixated on the bed. The doctor spoke, but his words seemed distant, as if wrapped in a thick fog. I obediently lay down on the bed, guided by the doctor's gentle touch. The nurse informed me that she would be placing an IV on my right hand, and the doctor reassured me to relax, promising it would all be over soon. I reclined on the bed, gazing into the bright light above me. Gradually, a sense of drowsiness enveloped me, and before I knew it, I slipped into a deep slumber.

When I awoke, I found myself in a room secluded by curtains. Faint conversations drifted in from the nearby area. As I attempted to move, I overheard the voices hushed, and a nurse entered the room. She asked how I was feeling and encouraged me to take my time. Gesturing toward the chair, she informed me that my clothes were placed there, advising me to get dressed when I was ready. Feeling an urgency to leave, I waited for her to exit before hastily slipping into my clothes. Discharge papers awaited me, a stark reminder of the choice I had made. With a heavy heart, I stepped out into the waiting area, feeling the weight of judgmental gazes upon me. It appears everyone knew the weight of guilt I carried within. Walking out of the building and into Jackie's truck, neither of us uttered a word. Silence enveloped us, and I couldn't bring myself to break it. Later, I discovered that the funds for my procedure were, in fact, provided by the county—assuming Ebony pocketed the money given to her by Brad's father. Who knows. Upon arriving back at Ebony's place, I noticed Brad and Wayne moving all my belongings upstairs into Steph's room. No one said a word to me, not even Ebony. I sat on the edge of the bed as they brought in my clothes, staring down at them. It was then that I noticed a small scar on my vein, a reminder of where the IV had been placed. My fingers gently traced over the mark as I continued to unpack and put my clothes away in the dressers, my heart heavy with a mixture of sorrow and regret.

EIGHT

As days turned into weeks, I found myself retreating to the confines of my room more often than before. A dark cloud of depression seemed to settle over my mind, weighing me down with its suffocating grip. Ms. Ebony's promises of adoption faded into distant echoes, and I no longer held onto the hope that it would ever become a reality. My battle with suicidal thoughts intensified, and I found solace in the familiar pain of self-inflicted cuts. This time, however, I took extra precautions to ensure that my secret remained hidden from prying eyes. I continued to take my medications, including the one that helped me sleep, but they were no longer supervised like they had been in previous clinics. Instead, they sat quietly in the kitchen cabinet, easily accessible. In a moment of desperation, I decided to consume half the bottle, hoping that it would bring me peace from the torment. I stumbled back to my room, the effects of the medication already taking hold, my memory hazy and fragmented. Ebony entered my room, as she questioned whether I had attempted to overdose. She warned me that if that were the case, she would have to take the necessary steps to have me involuntarily admitted. My weakened state allowed me to barely shake my head in denial, struggling to keep my heavy eyelids from closing completely.

After Ebony left the room, I succumbed to a deep slumber, my exhausted body seeking solace from the weight of my guilt. I believed that was going to be my final night, closing my eyes with the hope that they would never reopen. However, the next morning, they did. Facing each day of the burden of what I had done gnawed at my conscience, leaving me feeling unworthy of a place in this world.

It didn't take long for Ebony to bring a new girl into our home. When I returned one day, I discovered that Gabby had taken over my old room, the same Gabby I befriended at VYH. We stayed up late into the night, catching up on lost time and sharing the events that had unfolded in our lives. It was during that conversation for the first time, I finally found the courage to speak about my abortion. Gabby's disappointment was relatable, and she even joked about getting pregnant just to spite Ms. Ebony.

I introduced Gabby to the people I knew, hoping to provide her with a sense of belonging and connection. However, a twist occurred when Gabby developed a crush on one of my close friends. When he made it clear that he wasn't interested in her, I returned home to find Gabby waiting for me, seething with anger. Without any restraint, she unleashed a barrage of accusations, blaming me for supposedly meddling in her "love life." I attempted to explain, but my words were drowned out by her relentless shouting.

Ebony descended the stairs, drawn by the commotion, and joined in the accusations, claiming that I had deliberately orchestrated this situation to provoke her. The shock and disbelief overwhelmed me. Unable to bear the weight of their accusations any longer, I turned my back on them and ascended the stairs.

I made my way up the stairs, attempting to distance myself from the escalating confrontation. But Gabby, fueled by anger, grabbed my bag to strike me. Our height difference worked in my favor, and her swing missed its mark. Determined to avoid a physical altercation, I continued up the stairs, hoping that Ms. Ebony would intervene and put an end to this chaos. However, Gabby's aggression persisted, and our fighting began.

I ended up on the ground and Gabby's hands tightening around my throat. In that moment I made eye contact with Ms. Ebony, who stood as a silent witness, choosing not to intervene. It became clear that there would be no interference summoning the strength I had left, I began to swing back at Gabby, it was at that moment Ms. Ebony finally spoke, uttering the words, "Okay, Gabby, that's enough."

Gabby released her hold on me, and I struggled to catch my breath. Amid the chaos, I heard Steph's laughter echoing loudly, as she repeatedly taunted me, mocking my inability to fight back.

Fueled by a mix of anger and hurt, I rushed downstairs, hastily gathering my belongings before leaving the house behind. With no one to turn to, I began walking aimlessly, eventually finding myself at the back of my uncle's house, longing to seek solace within its walls. But I knew I couldn't go in, so I continued my aimless journey until I stumbled upon a park, where I sank down onto a bench.

I received no calls from Ms. Ebony, and I felt no urgency to return home. I continued to wander, eventually arriving back on our street. As I approached the front of the house, I wiped the tears from my face, summoning a facade of composure. Walking in, I passed everyone as if nothing had happened, retreating to the familiarity of my room.

Meanwhile, Steph and Gabby grew closer, their bond strengthening in the aftermath of the incident. Ebony, in her usual manner, planned a family trip to the Poconos, but when Esther told me she would go out of her way to make me look bad, especially when she visited to do her hair for the trip, Ebony had been eavesdropping on conversations between my friends and me, having the phone on speaker in front of Esther. It was only when Esther informed me of this, I became aware of Ebony's attempts to manipulate and distort the perception of who I truly was. In response, Esther deliberately chose to blend her expensive human hair with synthetic extensions, keeping the human hair for herself.

As the day of the family trip approached, I made it clear to Ms. Ebony that I had no intention of going. On my bed, watching TV, she stood near the door, engaged in a one-sided conversation with herself. My mind was resolute, and her words fell on deaf ears. Frustrated by my lack of response, she began to raise her voice, I simply asked her to leave me alone. Undeterred, she resorted to banging on my door, goading me further by challenging me to get angry. I recognized her tactics, realizing she was intentionally trying to provoke a reaction. Defiantly, I reiterated my decision not to go and turned up the volume on the TV, drowning out her attempts to control me.

Eventually, Ms. Ebony seemed to grasp the futility of her efforts and slammed my door shut in frustration. In her final act, she declared that I was grounded and forbidden from leaving the house. I'm not entirely sure why, but unlike my previous experiences in foster homes, I didn't run away this time. Perhaps I was simply weary of running, determined to prove to myself that I could endure and withstand challenges, especially since she claimed I would never graduate from her household. Looking back, I now realize that no one should have to endure an unhealthy environment, and I should have left just like I had done in every other home. But in that moment, I held my ground, even though it came at a high cost.

It wasn't long before the bond between Ms. Ebony and Gabby reached its breaking point. One night, Ms. Ebony returned home in a state of hysteria, sharing with Steph and me that she had been threatened by Gabby, resulting in a physical altercation. She informed us that Gabby was being taken to a mental hospital for treatment. Me on the other hand, could care less. Amused by the news, nothing changed for me and continued to spend less time at home, I would find solace in babysitting for her son, Jason, or spending the night at Jackie's place. While I was there, I met Jackie's son's girlfriend, who informed me that Ebony had consulted a psychic on my behalf. The psychic supposedly revealed my perceived strength, instilling fear in Ebony.

As the summer ended, I prepared to enter the 11th grade, realizing how quickly time had passed. Due to an infestation of bed bugs, we were forced to move to a new place. Ms. Ebony believed the pests had been brought in by Steph after sleeping out. Despite numerous attempts by exterminators and various home remedies, the bed bugs persisted. Another girl named Kelly joined us in our new living arrangement. She was known to a few people and was familiar with the area. Initially, Kelly seemed nice, she became close with Wayne and his friends, overall, her presence brought a refreshing change. Unfortunately, Kelly's stay with us was short-lived as she ran away. When summer arrived, I found a job at Burger King to support myself. In addition, I had become a part of the Big Brother and Big Sister program, where I was assigned my "big sister" Casey. Also, during this time Esther introduced me to a Haitian church, stepping into Healing Center, surrounded by the Haitian community, I felt a sense of comfort and belonging that I hadn't experienced before.

One day, while lying in bed, Steph entered the room and handed me my mail. Among the letters was a surprise—a check addressed to my mother and me. Opening it, I discovered that it was a check for $592. The revelation left me stunned and unsure if it was even real. Seeking clarity, I called Ms. Ebony to inquire about the check. However, instead of providing an explanation, she erupted in fury, berating me for going through the mail. Confused and seeking answers, I noticed that the check had a contact number for Social Security. I made the call and managed to speak with someone who confirmed that the check was indeed intended for me. They explained that I had been receiving these checks every month and that they would cease once I graduated from high school. The revelation left me shocked, questioning why this information had been hidden from me.

In search of guidance, I reached out to Casey and shared my predicament. Seeking advice, she suggested that I open a bank account to manage my finances independently. The situation revealed how furious Ms. Ebony was when she discovered that I kept the check, emphasizing that it rightfully belonged to her. Of course, informing Jackie as well, she disclosed that this wasn't the first time Ms. Ebony had tampered with finances. I informed Megan about her actions, and she presented me with the option of reporting her. She even mentioned the possibility of her losing the privileges of being a foster mom. However, for reasons I can't fully explain, I chose not to pursue that course of action. I instead had her repay me for the previous checks she had cashed, and she complied, every dime.

Casey accompanied me to the DMV multiple times as I persevered to pass my permit test. It took me seven attempts, but I refused to give up. I then became enrolled in driving school, where I diligently attended weekly lessons. With determination and effort, I successfully graduated from driving school and obtained my driver's license, granting me newfound independence.

With my money, I purchased my first car, opening doors to a new social circle, but it also exposed me to negative influences. I started spending a lot of time with friends who introduced me to drugs and alcohol. I found myself drifting further away from home, opting to sleep at their houses rather than being there. The rush of being part of their clique was intoxicating, and we engaged in reckless activities.

During this time, Steph and I acquired a new caseworker named Beth. When I found out Megan was no longer my worker, it came unexpectedly and hit me hard. I felt angry at her for not saying goodbye or anything to me personally, especially considering how much I had opened to her. However, I came to realize that detaching is sometimes better than attaching, and I began to accept that moto. More news came that we would be receiving a new girl, and to my surprise, it was Gabby. I couldn't believe that Ebony was allowing her to return after everything that had transpired before. As expected, Gabby's return brought back the same destructive behavior. Upon her return, she tried her foolishness on me. However, seeing that I was unfazed by her attempts to ruin a family dinner with my sisters her conflicts and confrontations were redirected towards Steph this time.

One day, Ebony called Steph and me into her room, locking the door behind us. As minutes passed, Gabby began pounding on the door, demanding to be let in. Eventually, Ebony opened the door, and Gabby rushed in, attempting to fight Steph. In a spontaneous turn of events, Ebony declared that they would have to fight since Gabby was relentless. I felt compelled to intervene, trying to diffuse the situation. Yet, Ebony insisted on allowing the confrontation to take place, and a physical altercation unfolded between Gabby and Steph as we stood watch.

Afterward, Ebony took Gabby for a drive, but when they returned, Gabby was no longer with her. Despite the hope that this incident would change the dynamic between Steph and me, it didn't. Steph's attitude towards me remained unchanged, especially when Ebony was present. The tension and animosity in our household continued to grow, eventually reaching a point that led to its final breaking point.

As I reflect on the past fights I had engaged in, none seemed to hold as much significance as the one with Steph. It was a fight that mattered, fueled by a genuine problem and motive to stand up for myself. But amidst the seriousness, there were moments that brought an unexpected comedic relief to the situation.

I arrived home to find only Steph there. The house seemed strangely deserted. I decided to wash my face in the bathroom, little did I know that Steph had other plans. She barged into the bathroom, demanding to use it while I was hunched over the sink, giving her a smart remark, I continued to rinse the soap off my face. That's when she pulled my hair, causing me to swiftly turn around. Something inside me snapped, and without thinking, I started swinging. Repeatedly.

I had a firm grip on her hair with one hand, while my other hand delivered punch after punch to her face. It was as if there was a target painted on her cheek. I was so focused on my own retaliation that I hardly felt any of her hits in return. During the chaos, I couldn't help but marvel at the absurdity of the situation. Not missing a beat, I looked her straight in the eyes and sarcastically asked, "Are we done? Because I'm out of breath." Her face was bright red, and I finally released her hair, walking away with a sense of accomplishment mixed with the realization that pride in such actions was foolish. Nevertheless, it provided a much-needed boost of confidence to stand up for myself.

After the fight, I went to a friend's house. As the adrenaline subsided, I realized that my hand was throbbing with pain. Concerned, I reached out to Ebony, and she agreed to take me to the hospital. During the car ride, tension between us escalated, and our argument reached its peak on the highway. Fueled by frustration, Ebony called me crazy, and in a moment of madness, I grabbed the steering wheel of her beloved BMW. The car swerved, and she yelled at me, pushing me back into the passenger seat. The words "You want to see crazy? I'll show you crazy!" slipped from my lips, surprising both of us. From that point on, silence filled the car as we continued our journey to the doctor's office. When I saw the doctor, he indeed confirmed that I had broken my wrist, resulting in the need to wear a cast for a few months. As he reviewed my x-rays, he couldn't resist making a joke, saying, "Were you punching the wall? Whatever it was, you must have been punching hard."

As my days continued to be spent away from home, I only returned when the need for clothes arose. On one of these visits, I discovered Ebony's phone left unattended in the bathroom. Inadvertently, I moved it causing it to vibrate. Once I finished, I went to place the phone back on the seat when a text message from Steph flashed across the screen. It read, "The monkey is back home." Intrigued, I swiped up, uncovering a string of messages between them, filled with derogatory slurs and expressions of satisfaction at my absence. Though anger didn't consume me, the pain of their hurtful words did. I quietly returned the phone to its original position and gathered my clothes, ready to leave once again.

During these tumultuous times, there were instances when I sought refuge with Chayes. She may not have been part of the inner circle, but she remained a steadfast friend, always there for me when I needed support. As I rarely stayed home, I found companionship in places where I had no business being, seeking solace and connection amidst the chaos. That's when I crossed paths with Lamar. Our conversations would stretch long into the night, often leading us to skip school together. I felt a sense of ease in opening to him, sharing my deepest traumas and experiences. The fact that he could relate to my struggles forged an even stronger bond between us.

Reflecting on my situation, I believe I didn't leave like I had done previous homes because a part of me was desperately trying to break free from my old patterns of behavior and create stability in my life, but I failed to realize the toll it was taking on my mental well-being. I was normalizing a toxic environment of abuse and mistreatment. I failed to recognize that by remaining in a place where I was neither valued nor wanted, I was belittling and disrespecting myself. It became clear that I was merely seen as a monthly paycheck. I suppose I was so desperate for a mother-daughter connection that any woman figure who showed even a modicum of kindness easily assumed that role. Unaware of the genuine qualities and unconditional love that should come with such a relationship, I perpetually sought something I had never truly experienced.

NINE

Finally graduating from Ebony's household was a significant milestone, one that shattered the notion I was unable to do so. However, as I reflect upon that accomplishment, I question whether it was truly worth the immense trauma I endured throughout my time there. The answer is a resounding "no." Recognizing this, I wasted no time in signing myself out of foster care, eager to move on with my life as if nothing had happened. I didn't take the necessary time to address the deep-rooted trauma, PTSD, and abuse that had shaped my experiences.

Without allowing myself the chance to breathe and process everything I had been through, I found myself navigating the next phase of my life without clearly defined boundaries. Impulsivity became a prominent characteristic of mine. Although I had been in relationships before, Lamar was the one who left an indelible mark on my heart. It was his support and understanding when I confided in him about my past that drew me closer to him. Even when Gabby returned (again) and reached out to him, revealing my shameful decision to have an abortion, he remained unfazed. He simply wanted to be there for me, offering the sense of being wanted and valued I had yearned for. With that one box checked off, we became each other's refuge, seeking comfort in one another's presence.

However, I failed to realize that in my pursuit of comfort and companionship, I was inadvertently repeating a cycle of toxicity—mentally, verbally, physically, and spiritually. The wounds of my past traumas began to resurface, manifesting in my relationships and behavior patterns. The desire to be loved and accepted clouded my judgment, preventing me from recognizing the warning signs that echoed the familiar pain I had once endured.

As I settled into my new living arrangement, Lamar's family initially welcomed me, unaware that I had moved in. I kept my belongings hidden, taking showers in the middle of the night, and we navigated our daily routines in silence. Lamar's mother was rarely home, so it felt as though I was just a frequent visitor throughout the summer. In those early days, I experienced a sense of freedom, or my own interpretation of what freedom meant to me. I quickly adapted to this new environment where liquor and drugs were easily accessible, and there were no authoritative figures dictating our actions. It was a time of youthful love, tinged with toxicity, yet filled with passion and intensity.

As time passed, it became evident that others in the house had discovered my presence. Despite this, I tried my best to remain overlooked. Even though it seemed like the home was accessible to just about anyone else, I still strived to contribute in whatever ways I could. When no one was around, I would clean and tidy up the entire house. Soon, my car became totaled due to my foolish decision of allowing 'friends' to drive. I decided to split the funds with Lamar's mother as a thank you gesture. Initially, I believed that these actions were helping. It genuinely felt like they had welcomed me into their lives. As always, I should know that when I think like this, I should expect the complete opposite.

Life has a way of revealing hidden intentions, much like how Judas walked alongside Jesus with ulterior motives. Though Judas's betrayal was part of God's greater purpose, the belief that he brought about Jesus's demise only served to fulfill Jesus's ultimate purpose.

Similarly, as I reflect on my experiences, I realize that even though I had hoped to build a genuine bond with Lamar's family, there were underlying motives and dynamics at play. Perhaps they accepted me to some extent, but there were hidden agendas and that I had failed to recognize. I failed to find the strength within myself to rise above the challenges and complexities of my past, at the time, I was Miss. Naïve.

When the summer came to an end, I was hit with two startling revelations. Firstly, I discovered that Lamar had lied about his age. Secondly, I found out that I was pregnant once again. Yes, talk about being "hot and ready." Feeling overwhelmed, I confided in Lamar's older sister, and it didn't take long for the news to reach his mother. Fear gripped me, but a part of me saw this as a second chance. Unfortunately, it was during this time that I noticed similarities between Lamar's mother and Ebony.

His sister shared with me that Lamar's mother had no desire to take care of another child, as she was already responsible for looking after his sister's son at the time. She expressed concern about her son's young age and his aspirations of pursuing a basketball career and how this would delay him. Even as I explained that this pregnancy wouldn't be my first and expressed my confusion as to why God would bless me with a child I couldn't adequately care for, her response remained unchanged. She then suggested an abortion, so I went. Returning to the same clinic as I had years ago was a haunting experience. Everything felt eerily familiar, reminding me of the past I had tried to leave behind.

The situation took an unexpected turn when I arrived at the clinic and, during the intake session, I mustered the courage to admit that I couldn't go through with the abortion. In a desperate attempt, I even lied, claiming that I had just consumed a drink before arriving, which led to the need for rescheduling. Lamar's mother was far from pleased with this change of plans, and the car ride home turned into a chaotic scene, with her screaming at me as if I had committed some outrageous offense. Lamar, seated beside her, remained silent throughout the ordeal, but I overheard him on the porch later, echoing his mother's harsh words about me. It shattered my heart to realize that he agreed with her, revealing a cold side to him I hadn't noticed before.

Feeling heartbroken, I left and sought refuge at the home of a mutual friend. This friend had played the role of a "sugar daddy" for another friend and I, always there to provide us with whatever we needed whenever we needed it. I wept uncontrollably, unable to comprehend how I found myself in the same predicament yet again. It appears my feelings and desires were constantly disregarded, replaced with yet another ultimatum. Amidst the turmoil, the only person who seemed remotely interested in what I wanted was this elderly man, but even in my vulnerable state, he insisted he would take care of me if I slept with him. Disgusted, I promptly asked him to drop me off at Lamar's house, only to walk next door to the friend who had originally introduced us. I sought solace in her company, staying with her for a while, despite being next door, Lamar didn't reach out. He seemed more interested in entertaining other girls, and my friend informed me of his disloyalty behind my back since they went to the same school. Finally, Lamar, in an act of love bombing, reached out to me, convincing me to move back in with him.

The atmosphere between Lamar and me grew increasingly cold. He became distant, and the tension between his mother and me thickened, which was a familiar dynamic for me. Dealing with morning sickness that would come and go, along with intense cravings, proved to be even more challenging. The transition from having a well-stocked fridge and the freedom to walk into the kitchen and prepare whatever I desired without judgment was now a distant memory. In this new environment, everyone seemed to look out for themselves, leaving me to manage with whatever limited provisions I could find in the cabinets during late nights when Lamar and I were hungry.

Randomly out of the blue to make matters worse, his younger sister's boyfriend started speaking negatively about my presence. The relevance of this was that I had briefly lived with him in VYH and we never had any issues. I couldn't understand where this sudden animosity was coming from. Eventually, I reached my breaking point. I caught him in the act and confronted him, which led to an immediate outburst from him. Lamar intervened, escalating the situation, and resulting in a physical altercation between the two of them.

Regrettably, his sister picked up on her boyfriend's behavior and began talking negatively about me as well. Their rooms were adjacent to ours, so I could hear every word. Thankfully my thick skin from previous experiences left me unbothered.

Overall, insecurities began to fester due to Lamar's cheating. He was no longer the person I thought I knew, and I wasn't sure if it was triggered by my pregnancy. So, the simplest tasks, like brushing my hair or my teeth, felt like insurmountable challenges. It appears everything had changed overnight. It didn't matter if I stayed inside the room, as his sisters managed to find something to say, making sure I always heard their comments.

One morning, I woke up to excruciating stomach pains. It was clear that I needed to go to the hospital. I turned to my friend, who called the sugar daddy for help. As awkward as it was, I had no other means of getting there. Soon enough, the doctor returned with news. He informed me that I had a UTI, which was treatable, and reassured me that my baby was fine. However, his long pause hinted at something else. It turned out that I also had Chlamydia. He prescribed antibiotics for the infection, but at that moment, I couldn't hear anything beyond those words. My heart shattered into a million pieces. I was left feeling confused, angry, and utterly foolish.

Rather than confronting Lamar immediately, I took matters into my own hands and went through his phone. The evidence I needed was right there. From the hurtful lies to bad-mouthing me to any girl who was willing to give it to him and denying the pregnancy when they asked. Eventually, I mustered the courage to tell him what I had discovered. A nasty fight ensued, and I unleashed my anger by punching, kicking, and scratching him. In response, he retaliated by throwing all my clothes out of the window. I sought refuge next door again, and she let me know about his late-night adventures of inviting girls downstairs while I was asleep upstairs. It seemed like everyone in the neighborhood knew about his betrayal except for me. I know I've endured previous pain, but this blow hit me differently. I hadn't seen the deception coming, as I had genuine feelings for him, and on top of it all, I was carrying his child. I spiraled into depression, my appetite diminished, and I started losing weight. I felt consumed by my own foolishness. I returned to him, trying desperately to understand why he had hurt me so deeply.

Feeling like nothing he said would make a difference, and sensing that his mother was biding her time to bring up the topic of abortion again, I allowed her to take me to a local clinic to determine the stage of my pregnancy. It was there that I had my first ultrasound. The experience left me utterly heartbroken, and I reluctantly went through with the abortion, but this time Lamar wasn't by my side. As I returned home, I found myself crying in that room, completely alone.

Lamar and I never discussed that day, and looking back, I realize that if only I had held on a little longer, things might have turned out differently. If only I had known that this wasn't the end, and that I had the strength within me to face motherhood without relying on anyone else's assistance. If only I had believed in myself and refused to let others, or my circumstances define my ability to provide and be a loving mother. Perhaps I could have created a different environment, one where everything could have unfolded in a different way. But my depression and darkness had blinded me, preventing me from seeing the light and hope that existed beyond my current struggles.

After the abortion, I broke up with him. It took me a while to recover from the aftermath of our breakup, but in all honesty, I'm not sure if I ever fully did at that time. I felt tormented, especially since he would openly bring other girls to the house while I remained upstairs, still living there despite our relationship ending. I mean, our bond did grow through intense and risky situations early on. I used to procure food for us, even a bed because, for a period, we slept on the floor in his room. Eventually I got caught shoplifting and he paid the fine with money he had selling drugs. I jumped into his fights, stood by his side during our multiple encounters with the police, quickly hiding the drugs during raids. It was often his younger sister's boyfriend or sometimes his brother who were the focus of the police attention, but I always knew what to do when they showed up unexpectedly. Even when I was handcuffed and faced with a gun being shoved in my face, I wasn't afraid because he was there, reassuring me. Looking back, I realize this wasn't a healthy dynamic, but at the time, I thought it was love. Or perhaps it was just a desperate grasp for comfort. I was so blinded that I settled for anything, even if it meant enduring betrayal, deception, and manipulation. Strangely enough, I never saw him as the villain or portrayed him that way. I understood that he was young, still in school, especially losing his virginity to me, he was now "hot and ready" I suppose being around him gave me a false sense of companionship, a way to alleviate the burden I carried, even though I was truly alone.

TEN

Okay, so I managed to get rehired at a previous job. Most days, I walked there, but on occasions when I couldn't avoid it, he would convince his mom to give me a ride. However, it was during those walks that I had some time to reflect and realize that I needed to get my life together. I was losing myself, barely making minimum wage, but it was enough to buy a new phone since my previous one had been stolen from the house. With so much traffic in and out, there was no hope of finding it or discovering who took it. I knew that getting an apartment was out of the question, but I had to start somewhere. I had to try. That's when I began researching housing options and came across a VYH program designed for foster kids who had left the system. They helped with finding an apartment and covered a portion of the rent, with the requirement of having a job. So, that's where I directed my focus.

I kept my head down and stayed in the room most of the time. The only interactions I had with them were while watching his niece or nephew. I ended up living with Lamar for about a year and some change, but it felt much longer due to the pain and mental abuse I endured. There was a waiting list for the VYH program, and it wasn't until my name was finally called that the intake process began. I was assigned a caseworker whom I met once a week. I explained my current living situation and emphasized the urgency of leaving. I knew I had to hold on a little longer, but then I lost my job. I remember walking to a park and breaking down in the middle of a basketball court. I cried out to God, expressing how exhausted I was. It was the first time I had called out to Him since the day I was placed into foster care on my birthday. Looking back, I should have known then that I didn't need a job or even to move in with Lamar in the first place. What I truly needed was to cry out to God once again.

Along the way, I had completely forgotten the essence of my initial prayer: "God, please be with me." The truth was, He had been with me all along; it was me who had drifted away. That's often how it goes - we get angry at God and question Him, asking why things happen, but in a way, He's also asking us the same thing. "Why did you go there when I didn't lead you there?" "Why are you in that relationship when I didn't guide you into it?" "Why are you moving backward instead of moving forward?" "Why are you running away from Me?" "Why are you dealing with all of this when you don't have to?"

It wasn't long after pouring my heart out to God a few days later my apartment was finally ready. I was overwhelmed with joy as my caseworker, and I went shopping for furniture and she helped me move in. Having my own place felt surreal, but I was incredibly grateful for this opportunity. Lamar and I were still not together, but my apartment was conveniently located just a 15-minute walk away from him. He had always felt like the black sheep in his family, overlooked and uncared for, and I could relate to those emotions. I couldn't help but feel partially responsible for the resentment his family held towards him, as it seemed to have grown because of our relationship.

Despite the betrayal I had experienced, my love for Lamar still lingered. I couldn't quite explain it. I had first met Lamar after a night gone wrong while still living at Ebony's place. That night, we walked together, talking about everything under the moon. He had a way of making me feel vulnerable and open. Occasionally, I would walk with him back to his house, and when no one was home, he would go through his mom's change jar. One afternoon, he stumbled upon a piece of mail that opened a door neither of us was ready for. It happened to be the same piece of mail Steph had given me, and Lamar was drawn to it because it had his name on the front and his father's name inside. He was confused and asked me about it. I shared my own story with Ebony and explained what it was. I encouraged him to talk to his mom about it.

Lamar was angry, especially since he didn't have many memories of his father from his childhood. He insisted on not speaking to his mom and instead, we took a trip to the social security office. There, a representative explained that the benefits were technically his, and he had the option to cash them personally, including the ones his mom had previously cashed out on. However, she would have to pay him out of pocket for those. Lamar declined the offer but grew more enraged, feeling that his mom could have done more for him. When he confronted her, a nasty argument ensued. Though I wasn't present, somehow my name was brought into it, and I became the reason for his discovery and his subsequent behavior. He was so upset that he came to me, expressing that he no longer wanted to stay at home. Feeling somewhat guilty and obligated, I allowed him to move into my apartment.

Lamar then made the decision to drop out of school after facing discipline from his basketball coach. Despite my efforts to convince him otherwise, he was stubborn and adamant about pursuing a career in music instead. He made friends who shared the same passion, and I supported him by providing what he needed for studio sessions and other expenses since I was working. His dream became my dream, and I poured my resources into helping him, going as far as building him a studio in our closet.

Meanwhile, my caseworker informed me about a program that could assist me in obtaining a vehicle. They would match half the amount for any car of my choice. Determined to achieve this goal, I took up another job that required overnight shifts. It was challenging since I had to walk to that job, but I persevered until I reached my target, and I finally had a car again.

I also started reconnecting with Esther again, as Gayu was away at college I sense that any bond we shared has faded over time, largely due to our lack of consistent communication with each other. I had become disconnected from Gaina's life, relying solely on updates from Esther to learn about what was happening in her world. Esther invited Lamar and me to church, I was glad to introduce them finally, never telling her about my second abortion. Attending church had a deeper impact on me than Lamar. I started attending services on and off. One night after service, one of the pastors asked me if I ever accepted Jesus into my life. Curiously, I asked how. He questioned, 'Do you believe Jesus died for your sins?' I said yes, and then he began to leap for joy, telling me I've been saved. Esther, standing next to me, was just as excited. However, despite my newfound faith, I still struggled with living a sinful life. I managed to quit doing drugs, even with the temptation that was present due to my surroundings.

Lamar began befriending our downstairs neighbors, a young couple. At the time, Lamar's income was dealing, I knew it was too close to home, but I disregarded my intuition. We all became close, and I even watched their daughter from time to time. They informed Lamar that the janitor of the complex, who was also their uncle, had a construction company on the side and offered to be his "plug" if needed. Lamar occasionally worked with them under the table, and I was just glad he was earning something more substantial than his monthly check. Everything seemed to be going well, and we grew comfortable in our routine.

However, my caseworker delivered news that I would be assigned a new worker who was stricter and more by-the-book. This new worker started monitoring me closely, seemingly intent on holding me accountable. Then it happened, the falling out with our neighbors, it took a disastrous turn when they reported to the landlord that Lamar and I were involved in dealing. As a partici-pant in the program, this report quickly reached my caseworker and prompted her boss to pay me a personal visit. Faced with the accu-sation, I denied any involvement, and since there was no evidence, he couldn't take immediate action. However, he did inform me that since my lease was up for renewal soon, he would arrange for me to be relocated to a different complex. I agreed to the relocation, feeling relieved that I could escape the situation.

I immediately informed Lamar about the precariousness of our situation. During this time, I decided to have a backup plan and applied for the housing choice voucher, and my name was added to the waiting list. While we had been careful to keep everything related to his activities in the car, I emphasized that it only took one slip-up to expose us. My caseworker visited me again, this time to discuss a women's leadership event she wanted me to attend. She brought over the necessary paperwork, and as always, I informed Lamar so that he could clean up and leave before she arrived. However, this time, he left behind evidence—a pack of wrappers right by the couch where we sat. Unfortunately, I only noticed them after it was too late. I received the devastating news that my lease would not be renewed. As a result, I was discharged from the program. The consequences of my carelessness had caught up with us, shattering the progress I had made and leaving me in a state of uncertainty.

After the incident I knew I couldn't go back to living with Lamar. Before Lamar returned home, he expressed his desire to reconnect with his father. I located his father and surprised him. We drove for an hour and arrived at a gathering of his extended family, who warmly welcomed us with hugs, a barbecue, and shared childhood stories about Lamar. However, his father suffered from dementia, and Lamar had to remind him of their conversations each time they spoke. Witnessing Lamar's happiness, I decided to reach out to my own father. He was sick but happy to hear from me, and he would send me money whenever he could. However, he eventually stopped answering my calls out of the blue, as well as my sister from his end who reconnected us.

On a spree of finding people, I decided to locate Meme next. I went on a search across social media until I finally came across her profile. I remember writing her a paragraph, afraid she wouldn't know who I was, but she did, and it felt like the younger girl in me received a hug from her younger self. I was so excited that I gave everyone her account so they could reach out, thankfully that didn't scare her, and we started talking every day bringing my partner-in-crime back into my life.

No longer employed, Esther, who was living with my uncle again, convinced him to let me move in with them. Living with my uncle was challenging, mainly because of unresolved conflicts between us. Despite the difficulties, I tried my best to adapt. I would still see Lamar occasionally, but not as often as before. Nonetheless, I wanted to prove to my uncle that I could be a different version than when I last lived with him. I took on the responsibility of cleaning the house, and when I wasn't working, I would go for drives to be away. It seemed that the less time I spent at home, the better.

One night, Lamar called me, asking for a ride to pick up his brother from Allentown, which was quite far away. In exchange for gas money, I agreed to help him, and by the time we returned, it was already late. Lamar asked if I could spend the night, and since it was too late to go back home, I texted my aunt to inform her of the situation. However, in a Haitian household, being an adult doesn't always mean you have full independence. My aunt was unhappy with my decision to stay out, and after a lecture, I decided to go for a short drive. In the meantime, Melissa called me, sobbing, so when I arrived back home, I was still on the phone with her, greeting Abby and Esther as I headed upstairs. Unbeknownst to me, my uncle said something to me from the living room, but I couldn't hear him from upstairs while talking to Meme. Misinterpreting my silence as a smart remark, my uncle responded by saying he had no problem kicking me out. Given the person I was back then, hearing those words was enough for me to decide—I left. I had only been living there for about four months. Although I didn't fully understand the underlying conflicts between my uncle and me, our stubbornness and differences in perspective always fueled the strife.

Living in my car became my reality, but I found ways to maintain necessities. I would visit Lamar's house to shower, but only during the middle of the night to avoid being seen. On other occasions, I utilized the free gym membership provided by the local county assistance office to have access to showers and deepened on food panties, luckily, I also found a program that would occasionally provide gas cards. My attendance at church increased, but I still hadn't fully committed myself to the faith.

Lamar grew concerned about me staying outside, so he allowed me to hide out in his room. So, I did, especially during my menstrual. The difference was that he didn't have school, so we spent the entire day inside. To keep my car hidden, I started parking it in different locations. Eventually, Lamar's mother figured out what was going on, but instead of being angry, she seemed understanding. Our interactions increased, and we started talking more with her venting about her boyfriend.

Living in such uncertain circumstances was difficult. After spending about a month back at Lamar's place, his mother had a breakdown. She called everyone downstairs, apologizing and expressing her fear that she was having a heart attack.

So, let's summarize this. Remember the STD? Even though I was healed it still resulted in a persistent cyst. Despite multiple surgeries and attempts to drain it, the cyst remained with me for years. I had to endure hospitalization and surgery on three separate occasions. Eventually, in 2021, it finally disappeared after a final surgical intervention. However, during that time, it caused me immense suffering to the point where sitting or wearing jeans became unbearable. The only relief I found was when I was lying down, which is why I couldn't join in the "apology party" on that day. Knowing that I wasn't comfortable coming out of the room, Lamar insisted that I didn't have to join them. During this time, I started to have vivid dreams, which my aunt told me were a way for God to communicate with me.

After his mother went to the hospital, Lamar informed me that she was deeply sorry for the way she had treated me. While his sisters were still downstairs discussing what had happened, I listened on the steps with Lamar. They began talking about their mother's habits, including her drug use. Their conversation triggered a memory of a dream I had about her, which seemed eerily like the events that had just taken place. Intrigued, they asked me more about the dream, and I went into greater detail.

Later that night, when his mother returned home from the hospital, I went downstairs to check on her well-being. However, when I returned to the room, she followed me and accused me of emitting a dark presence, likening me to what she had felt at her boyfriend's house. She started yelling at me, calling me "the devil," and demanded that I leave.

The situation escalated quickly, it was a frustrating and confusing experience, Lamar stepped in and quickly locked the door, refusing to budge. We hoped his mother would calm down, but instead, she unleashed her frustration by relentlessly kicking the door. It paused for a moment, giving us a glimmer of hope, only to resume with even more vigor. This time, she had her friends on the phone, instructing her on what to say to banish "the spirit" from the house. It was like a surreal comedy show.

Feeling desperate, I reached out to someone I had befriended at church. Thankfully, she offered me a haven, assuring me that I could come over. When his mother finally broke through the door, she demanded that I leave. Without hesitation, Lamar stood up and walked out with me. The snowstorm outside mirrored the turmoil within our lives as we drove down to Philadelphia, seeking refuge with my friend for the night.

The following day, Lamar's older sister reached out to check on us. She informed us that their mother had discarded everything from his room, ensuring that we wouldn't dare return. Left with nowhere else to go, we found ourselves living in the car. We would park in different apartment complexes at night, seeking shelter in the gym during the day. I kept my struggles hidden from Esther, maintaining a facade to avoid burdening her.

To keep myself occupied and maintain a sense of purpose, I became more active in the church community. I joined the dance ministry and eagerly participated in any event that was happening. I found solace and support among Esther's circle of friends and anyone else I felt drawn to. My pastor's wife (First Lady) ran her own child-care agency, and she graciously provided me with work. I witnessed the miraculous provision of God as my pockets never seemed to run dry as I took tithing seriously, recognizing the blessings that came from faithful giving.

If Lamar wasn't accompanying me to church, he would return home temporarily just for the hours I was gone. Although he didn't have to endure the hardships with me, he chose to stay by my side in the car. He would stay awake, keeping a watchful eye to ensure our safety. As time went on, we continued to rely on food pantries for sustenance. Lamar's grandfather always came to our aid, generously offering support and financial assistance whenever we needed it.

To pass the time and find refuge, we would spend hours at the library until closing time. Lamar eventually started working for his mother's boyfriend under the table, joining his cleaning company. The early hours of his work shift meant that he would drive to the job site, while I remained in the backseat, hiding beneath covers, still asleep. Despite the hardships, we found moments of laughter, and a sense of peace.

One morning, we woke up to find ourselves snowed in. Despite the challenging conditions, Lamar was determined to get the car moving. Unfortunately, his determination led to unintentional damage to the car's bottom, causing it to develop a leak. It became clear that we couldn't drive it any longer. Uncertain about what exactly was wrong with the car, I turned to Esther for help. She suggested a mechanic from the church who might be able to assist us. Recognizing that I couldn't stay with Lamar again, Esther proposed that I temporarily stay with my pastor until the car was fixed revealing she herself had once found shelter with him.

Lamar returned home while we sought the expertise of the recommended mechanic. However, to our disappointment, the mechanic proved to be unreliable and unable to diagnose the issue. That's when Lamar reached out to his grandpop, and he came to our rescue once again and managed to repair the car. Lamar shared with me the hardships he faced at home during the brief period he stayed home. His mother made sure he experienced the consequences of choosing me, and his sisters, who initially appeared interested mocked me and my dreams.

With the car fixed, we returned to our routine of living in the car. It had been nearly a year since we found ourselves homeless, relying on our coupon of the penny Whopper from Burger King, our savior in times of late-night hunger. Whenever Esther asked about my living arrangements, I would tell her I was couch-surfing. However, she revealed that my pastor was still willing to provide a more permanent solution by allowing me to move in. While guilt consumed me for dragging Lamar into this situation, I knew deep down that it was the best decision for both of us.

When I shared the news with Lamar, he wasn't thrilled. He didn't want to return home, so he chose to continue staying in the car while I moved in with my pastor. I made sure to bring him blankets and food, trying to support him as best as I could. However, our situation took a turn when we had a heated argument about me staying indoors while he remained outside. I stood my ground and refused to go back to the car, since we had no real plan, which caused him to snap. I vividly remember walking away from the argument, not realizing it would be the last time I would see him. When I returned outside, he was gone, leaving behind an emptiness that echoed the uncertainty of our future.

ELEVEN

When I first delved into the Bible, starting with Genesis, a mix of emotions stirred within me. Initially, I found myself irritated with Eve. I mean, seriously, how could she jeopardize being in God's presence? They had the ultimate all-access pass, something every believer today longs for, and they went ahead and ruined it for everyone. It was like they had one job, and even Adam wasn't innocent in this whole ordeal. I couldn't help but think, what happened to Proverbs 27:17, which says, "As iron sharpens iron, so one person sharpens another." Shouldn't Adam have stepped up?

Questions flooded my mind. I pondered why God didn't foresee that Eden was compromised. Where was He when the serpent was slyly convincing Eve to doubt what she already knew? Why did He even allow the serpent to be there in the first place, right amid God's presence? It reminded me of the story of Job when God allowed Satan to test his loyal servant (Job 1:6-9). My thoughts were: Even in God's presence, temptation exists. But here's the thing; Eve, despite her role in the fall, had a greater purpose. She was more than just the woman who took a bite of the forbidden fruit. She was still worthy of redemption. She was still worth saving. And if you ever find yourself drowning in the mistakes of your past, just remember this: you didn't single-handedly curse all of humanity. And if somehow you did, there is hope. His name is Jesus, and he died for your sins and mistakes. If you're alive, you are worthy of redemption.

Don't take my word for it. Go read the Bible, and you'll discover that you're not the only one who has been a hot mess at times. It's a reminder that we are all flawed and in need of grace. So, embrace your imperfections, learn from the stories of those who came before us, and find solace in the fact that there is a path to redemption and a Savior who loves you unconditionally.

So, there I was, given the opportunity to truly flourish and fully commit to God. It was like hitting the reset button once again. I found immense joy in being part of the dance ministry. Now, let me be clear—I wasn't the most skilled dancer out there, but I put my heart into it because I recognized that this was God's work, and I didn't want to treat it as just another hobby. However, looking back, I realize that while I was physically present, I wasn't always spiritually aware.

I had made the decision to be baptized, and our church was a tight-knit community where everyone knew one another. It had a strong Haitian influence, and we were growing and expanding. My relationship with my uncle started improving, and he was making strides in his own journey to become a pastor. Both he and my aunt went back to school, and although we couldn't reclaim the lost time, I cherished the progress we were making. After church, I would often join them for Sunday dinner, and as a new believer, I was always eager to show generosity to anyone in need. In hindsight, I should have established boundaries, but in the moment, I was simply caught up in the excitement of my newfound faith.

Pastor's house became a hub of warmth and familial love. He was a father figure to everyone, and I grew to love his entire family. Among the people I met, there was Anna. Looking back, I realize that my friendship with Anna was rather one-sided. I was always there for her, offering support and a listening ear whenever she needed it. However, the same level of care and reciprocity was not returned to me. I distinctly remember my sister warning me that not everyone is my friend, and during our nightly talks First Lady even co-signed that advice. But hey, they should have provided more specific details or else it would just fly over my head. This is precisely why I should have been more spiritually aware. Reflecting on this period of my life, I understand that my spiritual journey involved more than just showing up physically. It required a deeper understanding of my own faith and the dynamics of relationships.

It had been quite some time since I had been staying with my pastor, and things were going relatively well. I hadn't spoken to Lamar in what felt like years, I still thought about him, but that distance was doing me good. I stayed busy by volunteering for various church activities and being with Esther in her endeavors. It was during one of these volunteer sessions that I met Doug. We exchanged numbers and started talking frequently, eventually progressing to daily conversations. Honestly, he was younger than me, and at the time, he served as a source of entertainment, a distraction from thoughts of Lamar. We discussed everything—our dreams, goals, and our faith in God. It was refreshing to have open conversations with someone without the troubled past.

Some time goes by, and First Lady shared that she had been receiving letters from their apartment complex expressing suspicion of someone else living with them. I felt discouraged, not wanting to bring any jeopardy onto them. Luckly that's when my name had come up on the Section 8 waiting list just in the nick of time. Encouraged by this news, I went through the necessary process and started searching for an apartment. However, finding a suitable place proved to be more challenging than I anticipated. Most of the places I called refused to accept the voucher. The list of available options they provided was mostly filled, and my deadline was rapidly approaching.

Eventually, I did manage to find a place, upon learning about my situation, Esther selflessly offered me her entire paycheck to help me move in. I went to finalize the paperwork and pay the deposit. To my dismay, even with the holding deposit I had put down, they informed me that the apartment had been given away, leaving no units within the limit of my voucher. Undeterred, I continued my search and found another potential home. However, this place happened to be directly across the street from Lamar's residence. It felt like a twist of fate, but I made the decision not to take it. Finally, I managed to find another apartment, but the landlord was the same person who had previously reported me from my first apartment. My pride got the better of me, and I refused to consider either of the options before me.

Unfortunately, time slipped away, and I soon found myself running out of options. The deadline had passed, and my voucher had expired. My social worker wasted no time in removing my name from the waiting list and closing my file. It was a tough blow to face, but I had let my stubbornness and pride get in the way, ultimately causing me to miss out on the opportunity for stable housing.

In the midst of everything, First Lady received another letter. Feeling content and profoundly grateful for the season I shared with them, I came to the beautiful realization that it was best for me to leave. They demonstrated a genuineness that I wish I had fully appreciated our moments and expressed that to them—living in a two-bedroom apartment with three kids of their own, they embraced and accepted me as if I were their own. Never once did I feel the tumultuous emotions I had faced in various foster homes. The love I had yearned for early on, they effortlessly provided. However, I was too traumatized to realize it at the moment, as this had become a norm for me, and I quickly moved on from their life.

I was immensely grateful, above all, for their gracious act. I formed a strong bond with his children, treating them as if they were my own younger siblings. My greatest regret was not fully realizing the significance of that moment - an opportunity to dwell in God's presence within a healthy environment. Like Eve. Nevertheless, I was fortunate not only to receive their hospitality but also to engage in meaningful woman-to-woman talks, hearty meals, especially when Pastor would prepare my favorite comfort meal, "Patate au lait." It was as warm as his words and as nourishing as his soul, and he always seemed to make it on the nights I needed it the most. Even though my time with them was brief, they provided me with experiences that undoubtedly left a lasting impact.

So, these next few events happened back-to-back. Grab your teacup. As mentioned before, I'd have chats with First Lady before leaving and she liked to remind me to be careful with my company and provide me wisdom on relationships. All during that time, Doug and I became closer. Only two people knew about it: Anna being one.

Things started happening one after another. Doug opened about being a virgin and wanting more than just friendship with me. We talked it out and set a day for something to happen. Now I had no intentions of anything happening with him, it was just pure entertainment at this point. Before that, I went to an all-night prayer session with Esther. Towards the end, an ancestor warned me that people close to me might be jealous and that not everyone was a real friend. They even brought up my thoughts of hurting myself again.

A few days passed, and the day came for something to happen between Doug and me. Now, I don't know why, but I did it. I messaged Anna and said that it had already happened. Hot mess. When the actual time came, I met Doug, and all I gave him was a kiss. We continued to talk regularly, and I never went back to tell Anna that nothing really happened between us. I figured I could just forget about it. I deleted our messages, and that was that.

Now, here comes the twist. There was a gathering at a mutual friend's house with lots of young folks from the church, including Doug's girlfriend, who he never admitted he had. She came up to me, she told me they were in fact together, and I told her about seeing him and the kiss. More people gathered, and another mutual friend called him, putting him on speaker, he downplayed everything, and his friend made him choose, and he picked her. Doug tried to contact me, sending me a bunch of "I'm sorry" messages, but I didn't reply. Even after all that drama, I still had to dance in church the next morning.

Over time, I made friends among Esther's own circle. Esther suggested that I stay with one of her friends, and I did for about a week. However, the same letters started to arrive there as well, and I hit an all-time low. In that state of desperation, an old fling from high school happened to be in town, and seeking solace and not wanting to be alone, I met up with him and succumbed to sin actually doing something for real this time. The weight of conviction hit me like a boulder, and I turned to my "close friends" on social media to vent about what I was going through, although without going into specific details.

Shortly after that, Anna's brother, who held a position of influence in the church, reached out to me. I didn't disclose everything to him, but I did express my depression and struggle with backsliding. Since we had previously had conversations and he was one of the youth leaders, I saw it as an opportunity to simply vent and seek encouragement. As a result, I made the decision to step down from the dance ministry, although I still attended practices.

Fast forward a few weeks later, during dance practice, one of the leaders called everyone together for a "talk." More like an ambush due to it being the entire group of dancers there, his girlfriend stated I was spreading rumors telling everyone Doug and I slept together. I snapped and told everyone I wasn't going around spreading it especially since it was the last thing I needed at that moment. With no knowledge of where the rumor originated, Doug's girlfriend mentioned that Anna's brother had supposedly heard it from me. Without wasting any time, Esther and Gai both reached out to Anna's brother to confirm this. Esther called Anna's brother in front of everyone, and he denied ever hearing such a thing from me and clarified that he never said I said it was Doug I was referring to when I vented to him. Like I mentioned, I was discreet.

Feeling overwhelmed and frustrated, I shared the truth of what really had happened and our plans, etc. with Esther, as well as the dance leaders only. At that point, I no longer cared about explaining the breakdown in detail to everyone, as they had already formed their own opinions, evident from the side-eyes and judgments I had been receiving. Especially with the people who were still talking to me, letting me know their version of what was heard—from Doug and me being caught in the horrible act in church to a deacon walking in on us at night after bible study. Surprisingly, Doug was the only person trying to reach out to me. We made amends and no longer communicated. I created an unnecessary mess, and I can't even tell you the reason behind it. It was a heavy burden; I sought solace in venting to Gayu and opening a new door of understanding between Gayu and me. Having my back, no matter the situation. It was a door that I hadn't realized was there, as I had felt guilty for not showing up for her in the past.

During that time, I was consumed by my own battles and living a chaotic life with Lamar. I didn't want anyone to see me because I was in such a dark place, wanting to stay hidden there. I felt like I was fighting my battles alone.

Commercial break: I've come to realize that I often invested my time and energy in the wrong people in my life. I found myself seeking the company of those who didn't truly appreciate or value me. It also made me recognize the ways in which I fell short. I can see that my choices were influenced by my desire to avoid accountability and difficult emotions.

I noticed that I often gravitated towards individuals who shared similar feelings of shame, guilt, and trauma. Being around such people seemed comforting because we shared these burdens. However, seeking companionship based on shared struggles wasn't conducive to my growth and well-being.

I also came to terms with the fact that I intentionally distanced myself from my family. In truth, neither anyone in my family extended a gesture to reach out during my bleakest hours. Expect Esther who maintained communication with me. I scarcely recall any sincere attempts from them to understand me better; perhaps had there been, I could have become more open. Who knows, maybe being around them would have meant facing accountability for the lifestyle I was consumed by, taking ownership, and engaging in deep self-reflection. At the time, I wasn't prepared to confront these aspects of myself. It was easier to hide and avoid these challenges, even though it meant isolating myself or being around people who weren't good for me. Understand that growth requires confronting discomfort and making choices that align with your values. While acknowledging the past choices, become committed to using these insights to shape a more positive and fulfilling future. Meaningful change involves seeking out healthier relationships and facing emotions and challenges head-on.

Later that night, Esther and her friends were having a gathering at Mel's house, and I decided to join them, needing a break from everything. My sister suggested that I stay the night, and Melanie warmly insisted that it was fine. My attendance in church became sporadic. If I wasn't physically there I would attend online. I enrolled in community college in the area and connected with new friends, who lived nearby growing healthy friendships for once.

At Melanie's house, I contributed in whatever way I could. I helped with expenses and volunteered my assistance wherever possible. I made sure to clean up after myself, and since I mainly had night classes, I kept most of my belongings in the car, just in case. But Melanie insisted that I leave my things inside and assured me that she wouldn't kick me out after I told her about my past experiences. I didn't have a stable job at the time, and my phone was broken, so I started using her niece's old Android phone.

Melanie and I developed a friendship. We shared our thoughts and vented to each other. Despite everything that had happened between Lamar and me, when he reached out to me on social media, I gave in and decided to talk to him. He shared his struggles and frustrations back at home, and I couldn't help but think about what could have been if I had just listened to him and we had stayed in the car that day. I brought Lamar to Melanie's house after getting the approval.

When it was time for me to take Lamar back home, I was already planning to drive her niece to school the next day. Melanie suggested that I could use her older niece's car, which I had done before, and I could park my car in the back alley. I'm not sure why I agreed, considering I had my own car, but I followed her suggestion. I went along with the plan. We left late, and when we arrived at Lamar's place, everyone was asleep. I went inside to use the bathroom and left without disturbing anyone.

Now, back to that old phone I was using. It was a throwback phone that didn't charge properly. In fact, it had a lot of issues. We relied on Lamar's phone for navigation, and on the way back, I tried to charge my phone with the car charger, but it would never stay on long enough to guide me. To make matters worse, that night the exit I needed was blocked off due to construction. Of all nights, it had to happen then. Feeling lost and unsure of the way, I turned back and went back to Lamar's place to try charging the phone. I sent Melanie a Facebook message from Lamar's page, informing her of the situation. Since it was so late, I eventually fell asleep while waiting for the phone to charge. I must have overslept because I woke up to Lamar telling me that my sister was outside, waiting for me.

Confused and taken aback, I quickly went downstairs and was met with the disapproving gaze of my sister, Melanie, First Lady, along with two other church members in her car. Esther explained that Melanie had been worried cause she couldn't find me. I explained what had happened, showing them the message, I had sent Melanie. I apologized for causing them to worry but couldn't help but acknowledge that this situation had escalated because I had taken their car. If I had just used my own car, none of this would have happened.

I drove back to Melanie's house, retrieved my car, and headed to class since her younger niece had ended up going to school. It wasn't until I finished class that I received a text telling me that I had to pack my things and leave. I felt like a wreck, not because I had to leave but because it seemed like everything was turning against me at this point. I was just exhausted.

One of my classmates offered to accompany me to collect my belongings. When we arrived, Melanie was nowhere to be found, but she was on the phone with her niece, making sure I didn't take anything that didn't belong to me. Most of my clothes were already packed in trash bags, waiting for me except for a few items that I needed to put away. As I packed, Melanie's niece continued to berate me, blaming me for taking her car and suggesting that I should have gone to my uncle's house instead of Lamar's. She had no idea about my uncle's relationship, so I paid her no mind and let her rant on her own. My classmate helped me gather my things while her niece kept questioning certain items, insinuating as if I had stolen them. I had only been living with Melanie for a little over one month.

I stayed the night with my classmate, but I had learned my lesson about living with others. So, I decided to go back to living in my car and drove back to the apartment complex where I had previously found a spot to camp. It's funny how sometimes people offer you help only to later use it against you and add to the negative things being said about you. Some people just want to be part of the gossip and enjoy the satisfaction of saying, "Yeah, she did that to me too." Or "I tried to help her, she lived with me." That's why, if I had any money or resources to spare, or if there was anything I could do on my part, I made sure to do it. I didn't want to give anyone the opportunity to say, "she provided nothing, or did nothing." I always wanted to be more than just someone taking up space or another mouth to feed, that never mattered and at the end of the day that's okay, after everything I've been through, it would've been foolish of me to just now allow bitterness to enter my heart.

Lamar was aware of the situation and would occasionally borrow his sister's car to visit me in the middle of the night. He would gently tap on my window, hoping to convince me to go back with him. If I resisted, he would simply sit in the passenger seat and talk to me until his sister realized her car was missing. Sometimes, he would even bring me ice cream as a comforting gesture. There were nights when I didn't wake up to his soft knock, knowing that he couldn't slip away without being noticed. Abby, generously gave me her old iPhone. The daily commute to school was becoming increasingly challenging, and I was running low on funds despite applying for any job I could find. Unfortunately, I reached a point where I could no longer manage the commute, and I ended up not completing the entire semester.

Initially, my plan was to enroll in as many classes as possible, earning enough credits to transfer to an on-campus university. However, faced with continuous setbacks, I made the difficult decision to move back in with Lamar. His mother and older sister had already moved out, leaving only his younger sister, her boyfriend, and his niece. I did however regress into my old habits. It was during this period that I realized Lamar was the only person who had remained by my side, and we eventually rekindled our relationship. Lamar's niece developed a fondness for me, which I reciprocated as if she were my own niece.

TWELVE

Now, Lamar's sister had a new boyfriend, and he would often act as the peacemaker, attempting to foster harmony among everyone. Lamar and his sister didn't have the best relationship, and I had no intention of building any further bonds, despite my earlier pep talk to Lamar about improving their relationship. While his sister never explicitly said anything to us, we knew she harbored feelings. It didn't matter that I had a close relationship with her daughter and would occasionally look after her. So, when her current boyfriend crossed boundaries by touching me inappropriately and sending me multiple explicit pictures and videos, I knew I couldn't say anything—at least not right away. I had a gut feeling that he was aware of my predicament and knew that I wouldn't be able to speak up, especially considering Lamar's temper. I had experienced a similar situation before when Lamar's older sister accused me of "wanting" her boyfriend, when it was the other way around which led to Lamar making me wait outside her home to avoid conflict. I decided to keep my distance, feeling extremely uncomfortable.

After we moved to a new place, I eventually mustered the courage to confide in Lamar about what had happened, but I insisted that he shouldn't say anything. He respected my wishes and kept silent. However, it was both bizarre and repugnant when I later discovered that her boyfriend had finally confessed to Lamar's sister years later but spun a false narrative, claiming that I had pursued him, and he had rejected my advances. Especially since he only chose to spin the narrative after Lamar's sister had a lengthy phone conversation where we both opened and gained what I believed to be a deeper understanding of each other. Just as I thought our connection was improving, it was strained by the falsehood he introduced. That's when I truly understood the dysfunction, particularly because of her reaction to the whole situation. This revelation played a significant role in my decision to distance myself from their gatherings and no longer seek their acceptance solely because of Lamar. Finally, I realized that regardless of what I did or didn't do, I would always be cast as the villain somewhere in someone's story. And surprisingly, I found solace in accepting that role, which brought about a greater sense of peace in my life.

Now, getting back to my story, Lamar and I landed the same job, which is where one morning while I was wiping tables, a warm hand discreetly placed a card with her number in mine. When I turned around, I was taken aback to see Megan, who seemed to assume I wouldn't recognize her. I had no time to process the emotions; the encounter was so short. Still, it was a familiar face that I didn't know I needed to see.

Also during this time, we discovered the lights had been cut off in the house. Lamar's mother had left them with a hefty unpaid electricity bill and had no intention of having it reconnected in her name. She had also left them with some outstanding overdue rent. Despite the challenging situation, Lamar wanted to keep the house, so we made efforts to have the electricity transferred into his name. Unfortunately, no matter how hard we tried, we couldn't make the transfer happen.

Determined to find a solution, I did some research and came across a program that assists with move-in costs. At that time, the only apartment we could find was beyond our budget. So, we both put in as many hours as we could. Lamar enjoyed the job, but I, on the other hand, despised it. It wasn't because of the work itself, but rather the toxic environment. I worked tirelessly only to be mistreated by one of the supervisors, and when I escalated the issue, nothing was done about it. Eventually, I reached my breaking point and decided to quit, causing Lamar to also quit. The silver lining of my time there was reconnecting with Megan.

I assumed I had the capability to find a job anywhere, but shortly after leaving, my car started experiencing issues that were beyond repair, and we simply didn't have the funds to fix it. So, we made the difficult decision to sell it for scrap and used the money towards paying the rent. Lamar managed to find another job through a temporary agency, and his mother would drive him to work every day. I felt guilty for staying home while we struggled to keep food in the fridge. During this time, I began contemplating a backup plan.

I started walking to various apartment complexes that were based on income qualifications, searching for a potential housing option. Finally, I found one that had a waiting list. In the meantime, I applied to numerous jobs and eagerly awaited callbacks. Lamar was doing his best to cover the rent, although we were gradually falling behind. He really stepped up to the challenge. However, our rent was too high, and if I didn't secure a job soon, we wouldn't be able to sustain ourselves much longer. Exhausting all options for rental assistance, my fears became reality when Lamar was let go from his job due to absences, and the eviction notice arrived.

Only then was I able to secure employment. We spent the last of our resources on a car to transport our belongings, but I had a plan in mind for Lamar to apply for the same housing program I had previously used, so he could obtain his own apartment. In the meantime, his mother allowed us to stay with her in her new apartment, which happened to be the same one I had lived in during my time in the VYH program. It was a peculiar twist of fate, but it felt somewhat comforting to be back in a familiar space. We slept on the floor and patiently waited for his name to be called for the program.

We hadn't even been there for a full week when his mother started pressuring Lamar for rent money knowing he wasn't working. Initially, I didn't mind contributing, but her behavior took a negative turn and she started to belittle me. Was I surprised? Not really. I've come to expect people to be true to themselves. Despite Lamar's reluctance, as I was saving every penny, I convinced him that our stay would only be less than a month. And true to my word, we were able to secure an apartment through the program in his name, and we moved into a new place.

I gradually began returning to church, especially when Esther asked me to join her. However, I also started seeking my own path in building a personal relationship with God. Meanwhile, in the housing program, Lamar no longer had to pay rent, and thankfully, he had a caseworker who was laid-back and understanding. Yet, despite all we had been through, our past still seemed to trigger conflicts between us. It became toxic once again. Lamar grew increasingly possessive and would constantly accuse me of things I hadn't done, which I recognized as his own guilt projecting onto me. Due to that painful cyst, I was traumatized taking sex completely off the table this time, and it felt like we were constantly at odds.

I tried to overlook these issues because we had come so far, and I genuinely wanted to grow and mature together with him. I began to pursue acting and grew a passion for it. Esther provided an opportunity for me to speak at a foster home where she worked. It was during this experience that I realized I enjoyed public speaking as well, especially when the message was uplifting. It resonated with me because I had doubted whether I still had any positivity or uplifting words within me. I started applying for casting opportunities, and I received my first callback for a speaking engagement in New York City, where I would be discussing body positivity. I took a day off from work, and we drove to New York. Despite the petty argument Lamar and I had during the trip, it turned out to be the best experience of my life. I was determined that this would be something I would achieve and become successful in. We ended up spending the night in the car just so I could attend.

Around this time, Esther was preparing to get married, and since I had sporadic contact with Meme, I decided to invite her as a surprise wedding gift. I made all the arrangements for her to come down just in time for the wedding. It was bittersweet for the three of us to be together again, and everyone was overwhelmed with joy to see Meme.

Esther continued to be supportive of my acting career, even letting me use her car to attend auditions. When I landed my first official role, Lamar would accompany me every weekend as we drove down for my scenes. However, Lamar's jealousy towards my castmates grew to the point where it became problematic. He was overprotective, but I didn't see it as harmful initially, considering all we had been through together. But it escalated to the point where we would fight on the way home if I interacted with someone for slightly longer than he deemed appropriate. Eventually, I started going to auditions without him.

As Lamar started reverting to his old ways, becoming cold again, I became tired of the situation and decided I needed to get away. I made the decision to fully focus on my acting career and planned to move to Atlanta. I quit my job and began searching for a place to live. Coincidentally, my name was called from the waiting list for the income-based complex I had applied to a few years back. I decided to move in, and to add to the irony, it was located down the street from Lamar's place, within walking distance. Looking back, I realize that it may not have been the best decision.

While actively auditioning, I received a call to fly to LA to participate in a reality show. It was an all-expenses-paid trip, and I had the opportunity to bring someone with me. Doors were opening quickly for me, as I received another opportunity in Atlanta. I knew it would be a great opportunity for both me and Lamar, as he was still pursuing his music career, and I believed it would provide valuable exposure for him. However, he didn't seem as enthusiastic as I was initially. He downplayed the opportunity, but eventually agreed to come with me. Despite a few petty fights along the way, I knew that LA was where I wanted to be.

The show coincided with the onset of the pandemic, so just as it seemed like I was making progress, everything came to a halt. However, during this time, I started writing. Esther and Gayu had boys by now, and my love for them inspired me to write a children's book for them. I had always felt like I had missed my chance to be a mother, and at one point, I didn't even think I deserved to be one. But the small moments I shared with them touched me deeply. They brought me a sense of unconditional love and acceptance, invading my heart and revealing a part of me I didn't know existed.

Although Lamar was still living down the street, the program only lasted for a year, and he eventually had to take over the lease fully. Meanwhile, Meme called me in tears, explaining that she could no longer stay in Miami and was driving to Pennsylvania. I stayed in contact with her throughout her journey, offering support and whatever she needed without asking too many questions. When she finally arrived, she stayed with Esther, but they clashed frequently. Meme was trying to find her own apartment, and that's when I suggested to Lamar that she could be added to the lease of his apartment. Initially, he was hesitant, but I thought it would be helpful for them, so he agreed, and she moved in. Lamar paid what he owed and decided to give her the apartment entirely, no longer wanting to live there himself. Meme started working towards having only her name on the lease, and although it took time to remove Lamar's name, she seemed happier and was doing better. She did end up losing the car she drove down with, but Lamar gave her his old car when he saw his dream car one morning. Unplanned, I went half on the purchase with him, and it was registered in my name since he didn't have a license yet due to his record. I advised Meme to be open and honest if she ever fell behind on payments.

Unfortunately, it wasn't long before Meme started falling behind on rent, and Lamar was notified. After not hearing from her for days, I decided to visit her. To my surprise, I was greeted at the door by two strangers who refused to let me in. One of them threatened me with a gun if I didn't leave. When I finally heard back from Meme, she was angry at me for involving the police. She began texting Abby with insults about me, even threatening to kill me if I harmed her sister and her sister's boyfriend. Meme left without saying anything to us, and they were both evicted since both of their names were on the lease. I felt more disappointed than hurt. Finally, having my little sister back only to have her treat me like a stranger was difficult to accept. Esther assured me that she would stay in contact with Meme. Although we started talking again at family gatherings, she eventually moved away with her boyfriend and his family, and I just prayed that she wasn't going through a situation like I experienced.

Once again, I felt guilty, and if Lamar wasn't at his mom's house, he was at mine. Despite our efforts to reconcile, our relationship had been through so much that the wounds went unattended, causing deep-seated trust issues. Lamar continued making wild accusations of me sleeping with other men, and his behavior became unpredictable. Some days, I didn't know who I would wake up to. I saw him giving the love I desired to others before me. He was also mourning the death of our mutual friend from a few years back and resorted to unhealthy outlets to cope. He started projecting the hurtful actions of his family onto our relationship, and at times, I felt like his punching bag. The hurtful things he said resembled what his family had once said about me.

During this time, I noticed that the closer I drew to God, the further Lamar and I drifted apart. Despite knowing this, I continued to compromise because I didn't want to turn my back on him and because I still hoped we could grow together. However, it became an issue when I was exposed to things I was no longer attracted to, such as smoking. Lamar occasionally went to church with me, and I thought it would help, especially when my pastor spoke to him. But like me, his transformation didn't happen overnight. I tried to communicate with him, sharing the season I was in, my desire to pursue God fully, and my overall aspirations in life, but it never seemed to resonate with him. I began feeling the weight of maintaining responsibilities alone, from bills to rent, and more. I had always been considerate of Lamar's financial situation, providing for him when he was down, but it seemed like basic house chores were asking too much of him at that moment.

As I grew and my eyes opened, I realized that at that time, he couldn't be the partner I needed him to be. I noticed that the more I compromised for him, the more I neglected my own needs and my relationship with God. I didn't want to move forward without him, but I also didn't want to hold myself back. After another nasty outburst of past accusations, I felt drained and empty. I realized that I had poured so much into supporting Lamar's vision, goals, and ideas that I had forgotten about my own.

So, I made the difficult decision to limit our interactions. It wasn't easy, and Lamar didn't take it well. His outbursts were hurtful, but deep down, I knew he was never a bad person. I just had the unhealed version of him, as he was dealing with his own trauma, much like I once did. I wanted him to find happiness, but it seemed that at that time, his vision was clouded, and he couldn't see it. I knew that for Lamar to truly experience the work that God was doing in his life, he needed to go through the process alone, with only him and God in that season. Stepping completely out of it was the only way he would see it. But even before fully stepping away, I showed him resources and ways to stay stable.

I resided in my current apartment for a few years, and I must admit that during that time, there were instances when I strayed from my connection with God. Regrettably, this played a role in a familiar pattern resurfacing. It was during this period that I encountered a troubling situation with a neighbor who seemed to develop an unhealthy obsession with Lamar.

Yet, I believe divine intervention was at play as I had been forewarned through a dream. In retrospect, this tumultuous chapter in my life revealed itself to be a blessing in disguise, compelling me to make the decision to move.

I was fortunate enough to move into a new apartment, and while Lamar was no longer staying with me, he would occasionally drop by. I was reluctant to let go of the friendship we had, especially since he had been there for me during my darkest moments. However, even in our interactions, he would sometimes engage in hurtful behavior towards me, and I struggled to understand why I tolerated it.

At one point, he expressed a desire to move in with me and give our relationship a shot. He made promises of stepping up and improving, but his actions consistently fell short of words. Over time, he began to develop more toxic behaviors and habits. Despite my best efforts, his treatment of me grew increasingly difficult to bear. Eventually, I made the decision to help him find his own housing. He didn't want to live with his mother, so I assisted him in getting another apartment. Initially, it helped him; he seemed better, having his own space, and he was working again. It seemed healthy that we both now had our own homes, and for a while, our relationship progressed. Space helped us to the point where we almost got back together. As I embraced this season of growth, I continued to nurture my relationship with God and focused on my own goals and aspirations. I knew that by prioritizing my own well-being and spiritual journey, I was positioning myself for a brighter future, where I could make a positive impact and create a life aligned with my values.

I was blessed to receive another speaking opportunity, thanks to Megan. I had the chance to speak at Pennsylvania's Annual Foster Care Conference, making valuable connections with people. I met the director, some members of the board, and many other genuine foster parents, along with some of the foster kids they brought with them. This opportunity allowed me to share my experiences and insights, advocating for those in foster care and shining a light on the challenges faced. They brought boxes of my book to hand out during the conference as well. It was a 3-day trip, and I learned so much, realizing how much people valued my story and journey. That's when I felt the deep call to move; it was time for me to move on from PA.

At that time, Lamar had his two friends living with him, and he would often vent about regretting opening his home to them. Despite his regrets, he allowed them to stay until they found their own place. Meanwhile, I shared my plans with Lamar—not to renew my lease and potentially move in with Esther, who kindly offered her place while I saved for a month or so before making a move. Working a remote job, I had the flexibility to relocate anywhere.

Lamar then suggested I move in with him for that short month, comfortably within my comfort zone, I agreed. However, as you might guess, things took a turn. Not even fully a month into living together, Lamar wanted us back together, but I knew that meant living a sinful life. Instead I attended to other needs like household chores, cooking, etc., he remained unhappy. He distanced himself, staying in his room, while I remained in the living room.

Despite this, I introduced him to trading and investments, and he quickly excelled at it. During his job-hunting phase, I provided him with whatever he needed. One night, I discovered nasty comments he had written about me, and stating that my energy didn't match his anymore. My heart went numb, and after a few days, I confronted him, leading to a nasty fight. He became defensive and told me I could no longer live with him.

Ironically, after everything we had been through, those words were the ones that actually severed our connection. The next morning, I left while he was asleep, though he attempted to reach out, I didn't respond as hard as that was. I went through a tough time but had to keep it together when I moved in with Esther and my uncle, shuttling between their homes as I continued to plan my relocation. Being with them caused me to start attending church more frequently, so I just let God do his thing at this point. Throughout this period, I started praying for gratitude and searching for the lessons God wanted me to learn. I aimed to be a better person, and balancing my time helped me forge stronger connections with them. It gave me fresh insights into my uncle and aunt that I might have missed before. I enjoyed their company and my aunt's wisdom. I prioritized being present and savoring the little moments with my family. In this transformative phase, I opted to let God shape me, beginning with healing any wounds associated with them and letting go of my tendency to isolate myself.

Embracing Self-Worth and Finding Identity

At that point in my life, I came to a profound realization that it was not my responsibility to play the role of God in people's lives. No matter how much I wanted to provide, no matter how well-intentioned my actions were, if my efforts were not valued and appreciated, it was disrespectful to myself and my purpose to continue staying where I wasn't received or valued. I understood that it was no longer my job to please others or make them see me for who I truly was and the extent of my achievements. People often lack the capacity to acknowledge greatness in others.

Reflecting on my past, I couldn't help but think that perhaps I had stayed in certain situations for far too long because I had a point to prove. Maybe I had grown tired of running away, and I simply wanted to settle down and force things to work because I believed it was what I was supposed to do. Or maybe, deep down, I didn't believe I deserved more than what I was receiving. I had endured abuse because I felt it was my karma for past actions when I was younger. I allowed others to make choices for my body because I had opted out at an early age and didn't believe in the mantra of "my body, my choice." It seemed that from a young age, my encounters with "love" were meant to cause pain. Perhaps that's why I tolerated what I did for so long with Lamar.

For the longest time, I felt ashamed of who I was and the experiences I had endured. I allowed others to define my story, and I started listening to the voices that claimed I was the problem. I lost the strength to fight for anything anymore. But now, this moment, this is my way of fighting back. It's a battle against the negative seeds that have been planted by others in my life. I allowed those seeds to take root and develop traits that were projections of other people's opinions and expectations. It was then that I recognized this pattern and took the necessary steps to reclaim my identity. I grew tired of allowing others to jump on the "me too" movement against me, using my experiences for gossip and their own agendas.

I wish my family understood why I isolated myself. I wish they knew that from the day I entered the foster care system, the setup of some of the placements exposed me to a normalized sense of isolation. Whenever I shared my struggles with self-harm to my therapist, I was taken away and placed in yet another environment. I experienced being 302'd and placed in solitude. These experiences became part of my trauma response. But eventually, I took control of that response and removed myself from environments that intentionally caused me harm. Mentally, I had reached my limit and needed a safe space. I didn't feel like pretending to smile through the pain anymore because, truthfully, I was never fully present. And if I was absent, it was impossible for God to touch my wounded heart. I didn't want to be a fraud. I had too much respect for God and couldn't show Him the depth of my brokenness, no one else seemed interested in seeing it. I questioned, "What made God different?"

In this season of self-discovery and healing, I began to recognize the importance of valuing myself and embracing my identity. I understood that my worth was not defined by others' opinions or the traumas I had endured. It was time to release the burden.

So, I hid. Nobody seemed to notice because they were so preoccupied with asking me where I had been or why I hadn't attended certain events. But nobody asked me the most important question: "How are you, truly?" I didn't necessarily need them to ask, but it would have made a world of difference if people stopped thinking only about themselves and considered what others might be facing in secret. I am a person, not a persona. That means I am not perfect, and I no longer have the desire to be. Embracing my humanity means accepting the flaws and imperfections that we all have, the ones that most people spend years trying to hide. But if we continue to cover up rather than uncovering, we will never reach the potential that God has called us to fulfill.

I have learned that my worth is not determined by my performance. No matter how many times I may have taken steps backward, stumbled, sinned, known better but failed to do better, each experience has been a valuable lesson that has enhanced my understanding and performance for when I find myself in similar situations. Often, life presents us with similar tests but in different scenarios. I have grown comfortable with the unstable life I had allowed myself to be in. It's like being on life support but brain dead at the same time. If I was functioning and others saw me functioning, I believed I had met the mark.

However, it took me a long time to truly believe that there is life after the pain. It required a significant amount of faith. There came a point when I began questioning God, asking Him how long I would have to fight these battles. I struggled with understanding why I had to endure so much pain and hardship. But in those moments of questioning, I also discovered a profound truth—that the battle wasn't mine; it was meant for God to fight.

I realized that my journey was about more than just overcoming personal obstacles. It was about uncovering my authentic self and understanding my purpose. It was about recognizing that my worth was not dependent on the opinions of others or the pain I had experienced. It was about embracing my flaws and allowing them to be part of my story.

From that point forward, I made a conscious decision to focus on my own growth and well-being. I stopped seeking validation from external sources and started seeking validation from within. I began to understand that my true worth lies in being true to myself and aligning with the person God created me to be. It was a process of peeling back the layers of false identities, shedding the expectations placed upon me by others, and rediscovering the essence of who I am.

I started to prioritize self-care and self-love. I surrounded myself with people who genuinely cared about my well-being and supported my journey of self-discovery. I began to cultivate a deep connection with God, allowing His love and guidance to lead me forward. And as I embraced my authenticity, I realized that the pain I had endured could be transformed into a source of strength and resilience.

Through it all, I learned that life is a continuous journey of growth and self-discovery. It is not about achieving perfection or living up to the expectations of others. It is about embracing our humanity, learning from our experiences, and allowing ourselves to evolve into the person we are meant to become. And so, with every step forward, I embrace the beautiful messiness of life and walk confidently in the knowledge that there is still life after the pain.

Rising Above the Flames

I do believe that hurt can make us better if we allow it. And I want to take a moment to celebrate the fact that you are still here, holding on, despite the challenges you have faced. It hasn't been easy and being called "strong" has never felt like a true compliment because surviving doesn't mean you weren't damaged. Going through the fire of your childhood trauma is terrifying and uncomfortable. But as I look back, I am grateful that the fire didn't consume me; instead, it transformed me.

Each time I walked through the fire, I emerged as a different person. At the time, I didn't understand the significance, but now I do. I have learned that I must see myself as more than my past. For far too long, I was stagnant because I couldn't see past my shame and trauma. I allowed myself to become what people said I was, and I moved through life carrying my brokenness. I was robbed of the knowledge of who God called me to be because of how people reacted to my mistakes and who they thought I was. This led to doubt and uncertainty, and I never felt like I truly belonged anywhere. These feelings often fueled my actions.

The only words that echoed in my mind were "rejection, insecurity, burden, problematic, and shame." They became my identity, clouding my vision of who I truly was. But then I discovered that complexity doesn't necessarily mean complication. It became crucial for me to discern the environments I found myself in and the influences that were polluting my mind. I had to be mindful of what I was exposing myself to, as certain influences could lead to self-sabotage.

I came to love the saying, "Walk away from what no longer serves you." Our comfort zones may give us a false sense of safety, but there comes a point when enough is enough. We must be willing to step out of our comfort zones and let go of what is holding us back. It is essential to surround ourselves with people and influences that uplift and inspire us, rather than those that reinforce our negative self-perceptions.

Breaking free from the chains of our past and the limitations others have placed upon us is a liberating experience. It allows us to tap into our true potential and embrace the person God created us to be. It requires us to confront our shame and trauma, to heal from within, and to challenge the negative narratives that have defined us for far too long.

So, let us rise above the flames of our past and step into the transformative power of self-acceptance and self-love. Let us acknowledge that we are more than the sum of our mistakes and that our worth goes beyond what others may think or say about us. We are resilient, capable, and deserving of a life filled with joy, purpose, and fulfillment. The journey may not always be easy, but with each step forward, we reclaim our power and redefine our story.

Lessons from Moses' Journey

The story of Moses and the Israelites' journey from Egypt to the Promised Land is one that resonates with me deeply. As I reflect on their experiences, I can't help but draw parallels to my own life and the relationships I have encountered. There is a particular moment in Numbers chapter 16 where a group of rebels' revolts against Moses, questioning his leadership and disrespecting God. It is not the first time this has happened, and God is ready to destroy them.

But here's the interesting part: Moses intervenes on their behalf. Despite their constant complaints and disobedience, Moses pleads with God to spare them. This got me thinking, "God, have there been times when You told me to step back, yet I intervened for them anyway?"

In my opinion, Moses allowed the frustration caused by these people to consume him to the point that he disobeyed God. His actions ultimately led to him losing his opportunity to enter the Promised Land, just like the rebellious ones he had been advocating for (Numbers 20:1-12). The people's doubting and questioning of God seemed to have rubbed off on Moses, and it cost him dearly.

This realization prompted me to reflect on my own life. Who am I constantly intervening for, even when God may be telling me to step back? Sometimes, we have immense faith in people's ability to change, and we want to be a part of that change. We set high expectations and invest all our efforts into helping them reach their potential, even if it means delaying our own progress. While our intentions may be good, we can inadvertently jeopardize our relationship with God along the way.

We must remember that only God has the power to change someone's heart, and it may not happen at the same time He is working on ours. It is a difficult truth to accept, but we must be cautious not to take on the role of God in someone else's life. We cannot force change upon them, no matter how badly we want it for them. In Exodus 32:9-10, God even tells Moses that He will make a great nation out of him, despite the people's rebellion. This shows that all of Moses' objections and pleas were ultimately in vain, as the rebellious ones did not enter the Promised Land. Looking back, to me it wasn't worth it. Thankfully, that's why God chose Moses.

We must be mindful not to let our desire for someone else's betterment overshadow our own journey to our personal Promised Land. Only God knows the plans He has for everyone, and it may not align with our timelines or expectations. We need to trust that God's timing and His work in others' lives will unfold according to His divine wisdom. It is essential that we prioritize our own relationship with God and heed His guidance, even if it means stepping back from certain individuals or situations.

So, let us learn from Moses' experience and exercise discernment in our relationships. We can offer support and encouragement, but we must also recognize when it is time to let go and trust in God's sovereign plan. Our Promised Land awaits, and we must not allow our desire to save others to hinder our own journey towards the blessings that God has in store for us.

May we find the balance between compassion and self-preservation, trusting that God's purpose will prevail in our lives and the lives of those around us.

Okay, ya' girl just preached a little.

Embracing the Journey and Pushing Forward

The journey of writing this book has been a long and transformative one for me. I have been marinating on it since 2014, constantly revisiting and adding to it as I grew and experienced new stages of life. There was no clear ending in sight; I simply wanted to capture those moments, emotions, and reflections so that I wouldn't forget where I had been and how far I had come. And looking back now, I can truly say that I have grown in ways I couldn't have imagined.

During a particular time, I mention when Esther worked at a group home, she asked me to share my story. I attempted to be transparent, my voice trembling as I spoke. I wanted to be open, yet I still found myself trying to hide my wounds. But in a pivotal moment, I looked up and saw every girl in the room, recognizing a part of myself in each of them. It was in that moment that I realized I had to complete what God had placed within me. I couldn't do that without first confronting my past, my trauma, and my shame. Taking accountability when I was called to. It was through facing those difficult parts of my story that I could embrace vulnerability, knowing that it was something another girl needed to hear and know.

I had to learn how to use my wounds as proof of survival, not to diminish their impact or make them seem less significant. I came to understand that the magnitude of pain experienced is not a competition; it's not about comparing one person's pain to another's. Each person's pain is valid, regardless of its size or scale. I learned that living in my truth, even if it made others uncomfortable, it was essential. While writing this book, I contemplated what others might think and the narratives they might construct, but I came to realize that their opinions are not my concern. I can only speak from my perspective and vouch for my own experiences.

In each chapter, I tried to speak from the perspective of the person I was during that time. It wasn't just about the events or the people; it was about recognizing that after every setback, every blow, I somehow found the strength to rise again. Moments when I could have quit, moments when I even attempted to quit, only added fuel to my fire. I had something to prove not only to myself but also to the people who were counting on me, people I hadn't even met yet.

Sometimes, when I catch a glimpse of the faint scars on my arm, I am reminded of the moments that caused them. I am no longer embarrassed by them; instead, they serve as a reminder that I am still in the fight. They remind me that I cannot be easily defeated, and that some of our greatest battles are fought within ourselves. When we confront those internal giants, nothing can stop us.

There is someone out there waiting to hear from you, waiting to be inspired by your story. And that can only happen if you use what was meant to destroy you to build you up. This reminds me of Genesis 50:20, where Joseph speaks to his brothers after they sold him into slavery. Despite their ill intentions, Joseph recognizes that God had a greater purpose in allowing those hardships. He ends up saving Egypt from a severe famine and his own family in the process.

So, I ask you: What dreams are you holding back? What dreams are you running from? Those dreams may be tied to the lives of many people whom you might unexpectedly end up saving.

Throughout my life, I have learned valuable lessons at each stage that have propelled me forward into the next chapter. Whether through reading, hearing, or internalizing these lessons, they always came at the right time and became ingrained in my character. Applying them to my life didn't happen immediately, but I held onto them until the right moment arrived. I can't guarantee that everything will get better simply by hearing these quotes or phrases, but we all need reassurance. We all need friendly reminders that our current circumstances are not our ultimate destination. They are preparing us and pushing us toward what lies ahead. Before the push, it can hurt, and it may seem like things are getting worse before they get better. But I pray that in whatever season you find yourself in now, the gentle reminders below will aid in your transition and push you forward.

Allow me to share some valuable insights that I like to refer to as "free game." These lessons I have been gathered over the years, and while some may seem like common sense, it's through our failures that we truly learn and make progress.

May these reminders guide you on your journey:

- This too shall pass.
- Amid difficulty lies opportunity.
- You are stronger than you think.
- Let them talk!
- Every setback is a setup for a comeback.
- Keep going; you are making progress even if it's not visible.
- Embrace uncertainty; it is the birthplace of growth.
- The darkest nights produce the brightest stars.
- Your story is not over yet; there are still unwritten chapters waiting for you.
- You have the power to create a new narrative.
- Trust the process and believe in yourself.
- Focus on what truly matters and let go of the unnecessary.

- Leave the past behind and embrace the present moment.
- Replace unhealthy habits with positive and nourishing ones.
- Discover and maximize your true potential.
- Use your mind wisely and feed it with knowledge and positivity.
- Be gentle with yourself and practice self-compassion.
- Your past does not have to define you unless you allow it to.
- Remember that your worth goes beyond your performance or achievements.
- Nurture your spirit and take care of your soul's well-being.
- Don't grow weary of doing good, even when it's challenging.
- Learn to forgive yourself and release any self-blame or guilt.
- Extend forgiveness to others and understand that they are not defined solely by their past mistakes.
- Give yourself permission to rise above challenges and prevail.
- Continuously upgrade and pursue growth in all areas of your life.
- Work smart, manage your resources effectively, and build financial stability.
- Establish a daily routine that aligns with the lifestyle you desire.
- Strive to improve by doing just 1% more each day than you did yesterday.
- Seek alignment with your higher power and come into agreement with God's plan for your life.
- Don't stay in environments where you are not valued or appreciated.
- Evaluate your expectations and adjust them when necessary.
- Don't hesitate to seek help when you need it; you don't have to face everything alone.
- Take accountability for your actions and choices.
- When you gain knowledge, strive to apply it, and make better decisions.

- You can be content with what you have while still desiring growth and progress.
- Learn to say "no" when it's necessary for your well-being.
- Embrace and express your authentic self unapologetically.
- Honor your words and be a person of integrity.
- Invest in and pursue meaningful and fulfilling relationships.
- Make the most of your time and seize opportunities that come your way.
- It's okay to prioritize yourself and take care of your own needs.
- Define what success means to you, on your own terms.
- Love and cherish those who genuinely love and care for you.
- Manage your finances wisely and plan.
- Remember that what others think of you is none of your business.
- Find your voice and speak up for what you believe in.
- Respect your body and make choices that align with your well-being.
- Be intentional with your words and ensure they align with your actions.
- Set healthy boundaries and value them, honoring your own needs.
- Face your greatest challenges head-on, knowing that growth comes from overcoming them.
- Practice positive and healthy thinking patterns, cultivating a mindset of abundance and resilience.
- Discover your purpose and live a life that aligns with it.
- Embrace new experiences and truly live life to the fullest.
- Take care of your physical health and provide your body with what it needs.
- Understand the season of life you are in and embrace it fully.
- Never stop learning and expanding your knowledge and skills.

- Explore new hobbies and develop new interests that bring you joy.
- Dare to step out of your comfort zone and embrace discomfort as a catalyst for growth.
- Read widely and expand your horizons.
- Revenge is the Lord's.
- Not every helping hand is a helping hand. Learn to discern the difference.
- Don't beg for a seat when God has an entire table prepared specifically for you.
- Listen to your body and rest when you need to recharge and rejuvenate.
- Be mindful of your words and actions, as they have power and impact.
- Believe in yourself, even when things don't seem to make sense.
- Not everything needs to be shared; choose wisely whom you confide in.
- Protect your innermost treasures and don't waste them on those.
- Live a life of gratitude and count your blessings every day.

I hope these reminders provide you with the strength and encouragement you need to push forward, embrace your journey, and keep dreaming. Remember, this is not the end—your best days are still ahead of you.

Dear Inner Child,

I want you to know how incredibly proud I am of you. Despite all the pain, hurt, and neglect that you endured, you found the strength within to heal and grow. You took those painful experiences and turned them into a source of power and resilience.

Writing about our story was a courageous step, one that allowed us to shed light on the darkness that once surrounded us. It wasn't easy to revisit those memories and put them into words, but it was a crucial part of our healing journey. By sharing our story, we not only found a way to release the pain that had been trapped inside, but we also showed the world that our experiences do not define us. Instead, they have shaped us into a person who is strong, compassionate, and capable of overcoming even the toughest challenges.

You've grown into a beautiful woman, and the world is now yours to conquer. Anything you want, you can have. Don't ever let anyone silence you again. Your voice is powerful, and your story is important. You have the ability to create a future that is filled with love, happiness, and success.

So, my dear inner child, look at us now. Look at how far we have come. I am so proud of the progress we have made, and I am grateful for your unwavering strength and determination. Remember, you are not defined by the pain you experienced; you are defined by the incredible person you have become. Keep shining, keep healing, and keep moving forward. Our journey is a beautiful one, and I am honored to be a part of it.

With love and admiration,
Cindy Casimir

Thank you
read again